BY THE SAME AUTHOR

The Infidel: Freethought and American Religion
A Short History of Christianity
The New Shape of American Religion
The Hidden Discipline
Varieties of Unbelief
New Theology (with Dean G. Peerman)
A Handbook of Christian Theologians (with Dean G. Peerman)
The Modern Schism: Three Paths to the Secular
The Search for a Usable Future
Righteous Empire: The Protestant Experience in America
Protestantism

THE FIRE WE CAN LIGHT

MARTIN E. MARTY

The Fire
We Can Light

THE ROLE OF RELIGION IN A
SUDDENLY DIFFERENT WORLD

A *Christian Century* Projection for the 1970s

DOUBLEDAY & COMPANY, INC., GARDEN CITY, NEW YORK
1973

The Hasidic tale is reprinted by permission of Schocken Books Inc. from *Major Trends in Jewish Mysticism* by Gershom Scholem, Copyright © 1946, 1954, by Schocken Books Inc.

ISBN: 0-385-07602-9
LIBRARY OF CONGRESS CATALOG CARD NUMBER 73–83601
COPYRIGHT © 1973 BY THE CHRISTIAN CENTURY FOUNDATION
ALL RIGHTS RESERVED
PRINTED IN THE UNITED STATES OF AMERICA
FIRST EDITION

To Dean G. Peerman

Editor Extraordinary
    Associate-
    Managing-
    and, most of all,
    Co-

FOREWORD

American presidential administrations tend to create or reflect a national mood, a "feeling-tone," or a set of tendencies. These are manifest also in the field of religion. This is my fourth report on religion, in a fourth presidential era. *The New Shape of American Religion* (1959) withheld some consent from what was then thought of as a *moderate* religious revival in the Eisenhower era. *Second Chance for American Protestants* (1963) appeared concurrently with but did not fully share the generally *liberal* hopes of the thousand Kennedy days. What was called a *radical* reaction to the Johnson administration was also widespread in religious circles; *The Search for a Usable Future* presented an alternative to the utopianism in vogue at the time of its appearance (1969). This book reports on but is uneasy with the purported *conservative* direction in religion, a direction designed to parallel the one set by the early years of the Nixon regime.

A protestant assumption lies behind the four accounts: it is a good idea to keep one's fingers crossed or to drag one's feet when the "powers that be" project a semiofficial or widely applauded religious style. A catholic presupposition parallels this: it may be legitimate to affirm some elements of the national culture. But the Christian is responsible for building on the basis of his tradition's own inner resources, and not to be too much

swept along by the spirit of the times. Third, a historian's eye
is here at work. The historian is not supposed to be overly impressed by what is going on at the moment, even though he
may be called to chronicle change. "This, too, will pass." Finally, a tactician's sense is operating here. It asks, "Why tie
religious proclamation and style to the mood of the moment,
tool up to match it, and be left behind the moment a change
comes?" Some religious leaders have taken four quarter-turns
around the points of the compass during these fifteen years.
There are no more directions to which weathervanes can turn.

The conservative moment leaves me both impressed and un-
impressed. In the midst of blurry pluralism, particularist religions are prospering in the middle of a culture often called
secular; spiritual emphases are suddenly attractive. These trends
are noteworthy. Less impressive is the evidence that many supporters of these religions and emphases wittingly or unwittingly
prop up society's status quo. Their responses seem often to be
more constrictive than conservative. Conservatives are supposed to conserve, but the current religious newsmakers often
reject most of what Catholic, or core, Christianity has made
available to them through history.

Basic to what follows are two models developed by Robert
Jay Lifton. On one hand he speaks of Protean man, the
boundaryless and undefined creature named after a fascinating
figure of Greek mythology renowned for his ability to shift his
shapes constantly. Protean people or institutions lack fixity or
boundaries, and are marked by fluidity and flow. They are historically uprooted or dislocated and overwhelmed by a flood of
imagery from media. They lack identities or centers. Progressive religious forces often exhibit these tendencies.

The more visible recent trend, however, appeals to an opposite human impulse and is a protection against Proteanism.

People or institutions with this tendency are noted for "the closing off of identity, the constriction of self-process, . . . a straight-and-narrow specialization in psychological as well as in intellectual life, and . . . reluctance to let in any extraneous influence." When young Jesus people shout "One Way!" or new spiritual groups turn sectarian, they reflect this closed-off and constricted style. They display only an isolated element of Christian witness, or a partial portrayal of personality.

This book, like its predecessors, calls for a kind of protestant catholicity or catholic protestantism, a combination of Christian humanism with a responsiveness to the biblical prophetic note. If the call is in line with that sounded in the earlier books, the current report bears few similarities to its predecessors in other respects. The surrounding culture has changed too much. None of the chapters have appeared in anything like this form previously, but many of the ideas were developed in a number of lectureships held during the past four years. It is my custom to develop material for books through presentations at such lectures and to refine it through conversations with audiences at such events. In the course of three or four years, what survives goes into a book such as this one. Let me cite the names of a number of lectureships that were part of this process in the case of the present book: The Earl Lectures at the Pacific School of Religion; the Cole Lectures at Vanderbilt University; the Ritz Lectures at Winebrenner Seminary; the Weber Lectures at Moravian Theological Seminary; the Smyth Lectures at Columbia Seminary; the Cunningham Lectures at Austin College; the Ware, Lindley, Mayo, and Hillenbrand Lecture held, successively, at Boston (I.A.R.F.), Alma College, Rochester Council of Churches, and St. Louis University. I express thanks to gracious hosts and helpful participants.

Publication of this work also provides me with an opportunity to acknowledge the co-operation of Joanne Younggren, typist-secretary-colleague extraordinary, who has been a collaborator in these ventures for ten years.

This book is also my card of gratitude and word of encouragement to Editor James M. Wall and to *The Christian Century*, the ecumenical weekly that added me to its staff seventeen years ago and has meant so much in my development through these years. While I have never been more than a moonlighter in its precincts, the moonlight in those offices falls on an array of press releases, handouts, books for review, magazines for scanning, and ideas for picking and sorting; that array is probably unmatched elsewhere in American religious journalism. Religious journals, unless they are subsidized by or beholden to someone or other, have fallen into hard times, and *The Christian Century* is no exception. Barring the threatening ax of increased postal rates, it should survive and continue to serve, doughty and independent as ever. As a gesture of thanks, I am turning over the royalties from this book to the magazine; lacking fat cats, it has always had a skinny kitty. This is an effort to do something on my part. Its address—you ought to know—is 407 South Dearborn Street, Chicago, Illinois 60605.

Martin E. Marty

The University of Chicago

Contents

FOREWORD 9

1. *Always Keep a Hold on Nurse* 19
2. *That's Nice, Don't Fight* 47
3. *Open and Shut Cases* 75
4. *Clay Feet Clear Up to Our Navel* 93
5. *Without Boundaries or Center* 119
6. *Nearsighted Leaders, Blind-Siders, and Recovery* 151
7. *We Are Condemned to Meaning* 193
8. *Coring* 219

REFERENCES 234

When the Baal Shem had a difficult task before him, he would go to a certain place in the woods, light a fire and meditate in prayer—and what he had set out to perform was done. When a generation later the "Maggid" of Meseritz was faced with the same task he would go to the same place in the woods and say: We can no longer light the fire, but we can still speak the prayers—and what he wanted done became reality. Again a generation later Rabbi Moshe Leib of Sassov had to perform this task. And he too went into the woods and said: We can no longer light a fire, nor do we know the secret meditations belonging to the prayer, but we do know the place in the woods to which it all belongs—and that must be sufficient; and sufficient it was. But when another generation had passed and Rabbi Israel of Rishin was called upon to perform the task, he sat down on his golden chair in his castle and said: We cannot light the fire, we cannot speak the prayers, we do not know the place, but we can tell the story of how it was done. And . . . the story which he told had the same effect as the actions of the other three.

Hasidic tale retold by Gershom G. Scholem

THE FIRE WE CAN LIGHT

1

Always
Keep a Hold on Nurse

SECURITY AND STABILITY

"Ballast. Every culture needs it. Societies need ballast as much as ships or flying balloons do, to steady and to control themselves." The Jewish scholar Milton Himmelfarb was conversing with two historians who were critical of American religious figures who always reinforced the nation's status quo. He went on to say something like this: "You fellows are always expecting a Billy Graham to sound like a biblical prophet; you want him to upset things in the name of God. He has just the opposite function: he is engaged in ballasting. He helps give society its stability. He assures an uncertain public that its underlying values are proper."

Every large mixed group of people can suffer some knocking around. They can live with some excitement at the edges or the top of their society. But too much tossing and battering will only lead others to calls for heavier ballast. Other pictures come to mind. Society can be diagrammed in a shape more or less like Al Capp's cartoon creation the Shmoo. The Shmoo's motion is largely in its head. A broad middle and a leaden bottom keep it earthbound. The child's roly-poly toy, all beaming and motion-filled in the face, is ungraspably broad in the middle, and

burdened by weights so that it lands right side up when buffeted, and quickly comes to rest.

In that vision Mr. Himmelfarb was setting forth at a lunch
in Boston one noon in 1967, religion will normally help provide
some of society's stability and security. Religious visions may
have been born of fire and spirit and may have upset outsiders
at first. But those which survive usually pay a price. Later on,
the prophets, the critics, and some members of elites will
constantly be calling on religious leaders to attack many of the
agreed-upon values that hold the society together. A few leaders
will be upsetting, at least momentarily, but probably with less
force or effect than may appear on the surface of things. Now
and then, the most astute leaders will learn how to move the
ship or the balloon slightly or how to nudge the Shmoo or the
roly-poly without turning everything over.

The plot of American religious history in the past decade has
centered on the failure of most attempts to get rid of the ballast
and in subsequent weighting down of society by a security-
seeking majority. Those who talk about adventure or change
and those who take actions designed to bring about drastic
change, have largely if momentarily disappeared. They have
been replaced by people who feel it necessary to help ground or
balance the society with appeals to reassuring, agreed-upon values and ways of life. Groups that engage in ballasting prosper, while buffeters almost inevitably and invariably suffer.

THE FORMAL SYSTEM

Having faced the terror of change in the mid-1960s, by the
beginning of a new decade most Americans were ready to listen
to Hilaire Belloc's advice: "So always keep a hold on nurse for
fear of finding something worse." The nation was left with
what author Charles Hampden-Turner, in *Radical Man*, called

an intact "formal system." Some people call such a system an establishment, but it might be better to speak of it as a comprehensive "way of life." It is rooted in the fact that great numbers of people see the world in a similar fashion. In recent America, they did not like to see long-haired campus radicals or priests who burned draft-board documents. As they saw and rejected these upsetters, they drew closer together in defense of the world as it was.

A formal system will tend to promote a common sense of identity among people. The symbols of that identity have shown up most confidently on automobile bumper stickers. "Love It or Leave It" presumes to defend an America that does not need and will not tolerate criticism or change. "Register Communists and Not Firearms" forgets logic while it suggests that force at home can keep the hated outsider away. "Support Your Local Police" underscores that imagery. "My God Is Alive —Too Bad About Yours" suggests no need to ask disturbing questions. Religion has survived the questioners. Such slogans support a sense of identity.

The members in a system have a common purpose and a set of investments in the environment around them. They will risk little, but some minor experiment or motion is possible. Consensus groups need to keep some distance between themselves and other groups. They may engage in occasional venturing or bridge building. President Richard Nixon's carefully orchestrated trip to China was an example of how, when the time is right, a public will tolerate changed imagery, so long as it brings about no inconvenience.

Advocates of the formal system will set out to make impressions to confirm their own picture of themselves. Powerful America bombs as a "show of force." Citizens drive the long-hair youth off the streets in order to let everyone know what they will not tolerate. Now and then they may interact with and learn from neighboring groups or societies—they may shop for a few values. The need to rearrange the ballast of society may result, and some of it may even be jettisoned.

A formal system ordinarily lives by consensus and allows for only minor jostling. Only in a time of real revolution would matters be different, and then probably momentarily. No doubt, in Himmelfarb's picture as it would be in that of almost any "realistic" student of society, after a revolution a new formal system would take effect and new ballast would be needed and found almost at once. America in the 1960s, despite a few appearances to the contrary, turned out not to have been in a prerevolutionary situation. It, too, lived by consensus.

FREEDOM AND EQUALITY SEEM SECONDARY

Religion supported that consensus and added to the ballast. Predictably, about 80 per cent of the population could be expected to respond to polls in support of the assured values. When the United States Supreme Court in 1962 and 1963 struck down school prayer and devotional exercises in public education, almost 80 per cent of the people were critical of those decisions. They seemed to deprive society of some of its balancing weight. The sense that people were being short-changed spiritually did not result in any compensatory acts. Thus, Sunday-school enrollments did not increase. They declined. The polls merely served to show that people were uneasy or mildly enraged about the jettisoning of some of their ballast. When interviewers or pollsters regularly inquired about religious peoples' attitudes toward the decade-long war in Vietnam or toward demonstrators for racial justice, the opinions of religious believers differed hardly at all from those of their neighbors. More often than not, religious affiliation only served to deepen their attachment to the formal system.

Milton Himmelfarb was no doubt correct. It is more important to understand the ballasting of society than to pretend it away or to lambaste the majority of the people. Members of elites may enjoy themselves deriding the silent majority or middle America, the hardhats and backlashers. But if they are only cynical, someone else will come along and grasp what is happening, either to change the world for the better or to exploit the supporters of the formal system.

In many respects the world is not much different from the one that historian Carl Becker faced in 1932 when he spoke on "The Dilemma of Liberals in Our Time." "Time was, not so long ago, when the word 'liberal' went about the world in shining morning face, proud of its achievements, confident of its future. Today, none so poor to do it reverence, it peers cautiously out of doorways, shuffles along the shadow of walls, slinks around corners into side streets."

He spoke out of the critical university community. There people had the ability or the freedom to buffet and jostle society. Becker rued the fact that "at present the gods appear to cast a favourable eye on the common man. . . . Unfortunately for us [academics] perhaps, the intellectual freedom which we so highly prize is of little concern to the average man, since he rarely uses it, while the freedoms he can make use of are of slight value to him." Similarly, appeals for equality are threats to him. "What the average man wants, much more than he wants the liberties we prize, is security; and he will support those who can and will give it to him."

Religious leaders have learned once again that most people are not free to prize the intellectual freedom of Father Daniel Berrigan or "Pentagon Papers" man Daniel Ellsberg. They will not tolerate clerical defense of such disturbers of the quiet. They do not know why religious institutions should concern themselves with freedom of the air waves, reporters' freedom to protect confidential sources of information, or libertarians' attempts to ward off governmental eavesdropping. Carl Becker's average man can say anything he will find it necessary to say, and will thus believe he is experiencing complete freedom.

Equality is also an expensive luxury for that white man who knows that bringing blacks up to his status in the factory assembly line may mean a threat to his own job, or that moving the Chicano into his neighborhood may downgrade property values there. So he will be resentful of people who use the resources of his religious group to jostle the system. It matters little if this jostling is done on the basis of sacred symbol such as those drawn from biblical prophecy. "What the average man wants . . . is security." He supports those who give it to him. In that spirit the 1960s ended and the 1970s began, in and around the religious world.

If the promise of American life is to be fulfilled, if freedom is to be extended and equality enjoyed, future moves will have to be made with some sense of regard for the love of ballast, the support of the formal system, or the drive for security. Such regard need not mean that people of vision simply must acquiesce to the world as it is. But they must have empathy for those who suffer in that world's mixture of slavery and freedom. True leaders will try to discuss the points at which people show discontent with the formal system or give signs that they might venture within the limits such a system permits.

ELITE DEFENSE OF THE CONSENSUS

Spotting those places is a more difficult task than it was in the early 1960s, before the upheavals and reaction. The temptations to give the efforts up are many, disguised though they may be. While Carl Becker in his day could at least rue that day and hope a bit, many of the critics of the formal system have simply disappeared in the recent past. Others, among them latter-day discoverers of the leftover power of "the ethnics," supporters of the status quo, sometimes set out to teach politicians the lesson of that ethnic power, or middle America, by suggesting that its might makes right. Let me illustrate.

By the time of the 1972 United States presidential campaign, coauthors Lowell D. Streiker and Gerald S. Strober came close to saying that whatever is, is right about "consensus" America. In *Religion and the New Majority* they set out to show that evangelist Billy Graham more than Richard M. Nixon was America's foremost political leader, because he combined spiritual power with what Becker's average man wanted. "His description of America's problems, his rejection of extremism, his stress on the worth of the individual, his strong support of the work ethic, his suggestion that God has singled out America for special blessing and special responsibility elicit positive chords of response from an American majority which is deeply troubled but which desires to find a constructively moderate way out of the wilderness." They were critical of the critics and prophets and evidently moved by a genuine desire to help Americans find their spiritual moorings. The coauthors even asked for a one-year moratorium on any programs that "in actual or potential terms increase polarization within American life."

The romantic defenders of "the ethnics" and the spokesmen to and for "the new majority" probably contributed to the ballast in the American ship more than they helped move it forward. But they can be credited at least for trying to discern and to give voice to positive values in "the average man's world."

That world had often been overlooked in the previous decade by critics who took refuge in the academy, in the pulpit, or in the safety of institutional bureaus and boards, where they failed to notice their own security systems and personal support groups.

SOMETIMES MAJORITIES RISK

What many of the newer elitist defenders of the formal system failed to do was to look for the places where members of the majority might entertain some worthwhile risk. The bumper stickers, which seemed hyperpatriotic, may often have signified a bravado that covered up uncertainties. These uncertainties, once discerned, could be turned to creative purpose. For example, those who believed throughout the Vietnam War that selective conscientious objection was a humane and moral alternative faced difficult draft boards. But they often found that behind the façade of unquestioning patriotism, many members of these boards could be moved to recognize issues of conscience and morality embodied by some of the dissenters. Given the right climate, numbers of previously hostile people could be brought to see that maybe American families should be reunited. National reconciliation could better occur if society took a risk by granting amnesty to objectors who had moved to Canada or Sweden.

Patient devotion to detail on the part of some dissenting leaders revealed that not all Americans were inhumanely "anti-permissive" and in favor of the work ethic in so far as these issues related to some mothers on welfare. Of course, some political leaders know how to manipulate people, to cover up these openings. But the situations do offer hope, while simple defense of the status quo on the part of those who should know better will not help bring about a more humane situation.

No recent event better illustrates the possibility of altering the formal system, of shifting the ballast, than the one symbolized by the President's already mentioned visit to China in 1972. For a score of years China had been represented as the most brutal nation in the world. At times it had been pretended away, and at others it had been used as a bogey to frighten people. But when the time came for Americans to begin to notice China—in other words, when such notice was advantageous to them—the whole value system was altered, because it could be done within the context of security. The move was by no means based exclusively on deep humane yearnings. Commerce and diplomacy received priority. But in today's world one may often be ready to settle for the good that can come from long-range, as opposed to short-range, self-interest when altruism is entirely out of the question in any case. Suddenly China was viewed partly positively, and was permitted to join the human race.

Is the "work ethic," to take a second example, really believed in? At Holden Village, a religious retreat center in an old mining village in Washington State, we found in the summer of 1969 that middle-class families there turned out to be more divided over this issue than over Vietnam, race, or radicalism. Their discussions usually began with a defense of the work ethic by middle-class fathers—workaholics who were at Holden to see whether they could be cured. Many of their offspring, though it is true that they were sometimes artificially divorced from the need to see the ethical system from within, complained. In their eyes, it was precisely that system which had led to pollution of air and stream. It had contributed to father's ulcers, heart attacks, alcoholism, endocrine disturbances, and other Christian diseases. "Why support the system that's killing Dad?" The middle-aged overworkers were consistently surprised at the hitherto suppressed rage their spouses or children showed against their belief in and support of that system.

Unfortunately there is seldom a political advantage in questioning what has come to be called the work ethic. Vote seekers know that hard workers resent many features of a welfare society. They can exploit that resentment and stimulate politically valuable rage against those who are not in position to share the mixed benefits of the system. But religious leaders ought to know that in most spiritual visions, man is to be measured not only by how much he produces or how long he works; he is also to be regarded intrinsically, seen to be valuable also when free of necessity, at leisure, or when meditating.

Curiously, a part of the new attraction of China to those who criticized "permissiveness" or the weakening of "the work ethic" lay in the fact that China seemed to them to exemplify old Puritan ways and means that were slipping from much of American life. But the world seems better off for America's notice of China's millions, even if America may be worse off for the confirmation its grim-set-jaw leaders found in China's efficient, orderly, and routinized life.

THE TREND TOWARD TRENDLESSNESS

From these remarks it can be seen that the "ballast" theory does not commit a person to seeing or foreseeing a forthcoming Fascist America. Not all the dangers come from the far right. It may well be that Yeats's vision is coming true: "the best lack all conviction, while the worst are full of passionate intensity." The backlash to the lashing that the average man thought he took in the 1960s has not always been simply repressive or authoritarian. What might be called securitism is probably a greater immediate threat to freedom and equality than is the persecuting instinct or ideological threat. "Who's afraid of the radical right?" The supporters of the formal system tend to see Fascism simply as a mirror image of agitation from the far left. The rightist fanatic also is bopping the head of the roly-poly or buffeting the top of the Shmoo. Citizens usually see that he, too, has to be countered by their adding more to the ballast, by their further weighting down and rendering more nearly immobile the larger society.

By the end of the first Nixon administration, the result was a society characterized less by the old intense polarizations and more by a sense of exhaustion. Observers reached for various descriptions. The trend of the early 1970s was trendlessness; there had been too many trends in the previous decade. If the pace of change had been artificially accelerated in the earlier decade, it was resisted with compensatory apathy a couple of years later. *The Christian Century* chartered a series of articles on tension and polarities in American life. The editors asked potential authors what the price of reconciliation from both sides of various rending issues might be. Months later, by the time the articles appeared, the situation had changed so much that the opposite problem had appeared: everyone seemed to be asleep.

The gifted reporter sees and knows in his bones what the social scientist and historian later confirm through research. Such reporters were moved to call the early 1970s "the age of melancholy" in contrast to the 1950s with their "age of anxiety" or the 1960s, "the age of upheaval." How does one measure apathy? The lapel buttons spoke of it, in past, present, and future tenses. "Nostalgia isn't what it used to be." "I am neither for nor against apathy." "Due to lack of interest, tomorrow has been cancelled." A radio station announced that "apathy" would be the topic for the day's telephone call-in show. No one called.

The disease Chicagoans call "the Februaries," a spiritually numbing malaise, seemed to circle the seasons. Galloping exhaustion, creeping apathy, intense anomie, raging disappointment, enthusiastic failure of nerve, galloping entropy, all were observed almost a moment after the passions of 1968 had died down. The United States seemed to be an emotionally "burnt-over district," much as western New York had been after the revivals toward the middle of the nineteenth century. "Mourning becomes America."

Some thought that the prolonged enervation of the Vietnam War had led people to be unshockable. No moral outrage, no My Lai, no mass bombing of civilians produced effective conscientious opposition. The citizens almost seemed for a time to welcome the idea that President Nixon and his clerical friend would have to assume all the guilt for what the chief executive had done and what his pastor had allowed to pass in silence. The landslide election victory of 1972 temporarily confirmed the leadership in the course it had set. Why would such victors want to change the formal system or reduce the ballast? Opponents had been reduced to humorless whining— and who loves or is moved by a whiner?

Implied in these lines has been the assumption that a political administration sets a kind of spiritual tone for a society. The spirit of the Eisenhower years, the Kennedy-Johnson era, or the Nixon terms seems to have been set so early in each administration that one can hardly picture a President as having been responsible for its arrival. Perhaps by the time an election has occurred, society has already engaged in shifting or tilting and knows what it wants. In any case, the spiritual moods accompanying these administrations are clearly discernible. The President may have priestly functions. He certainly is free to use that "bully pulpit" of which Theodore Roosevelt once spoke. He emits subtle signals that can confirm the new status quo.

The Eisenhower years saw a mobile but anxious people seek security in conformist values. A revival of interest in religion then took the form of the building up of religious institutions. The 1960s began with a national liberal turn, with a slightly more secular tilt. This was followed by a series of strains in society and an eventual return to strong support of the formal system. By 1968 the majority of voting Americans knew what they wanted, and in 1972 they asked for four more years of it: ballast. The new national mood was set in the midst of the discontents and dissents of 1968–69. The inherited establishment, contrary to many prophecies, had not been revolutionized. Some of the spiritual heroes of the 1950s were trotted out on stage once more, or replaced by heirs in their own lineage. The preoccupation with efficiency and impersonal administration that the French writer Simone Weil had prophesied would one day enslave man had outlasted the dissenters' visions. A simple hedonism survived in a two-car, one-boat culture. The fear of something worse had led to holding on to nurse.

The revelation in 1973 of high-level corruption in the Nixon administration presented a test for the formal system. Significantly, the earliest and most consistent criticism of White House practices came from the right: from Constitutional conservative Senator Sam Ervin; from rightist Senator Barry Goldwater; from columnists James J. Kilpatrick and William F. Buckley, Jr. They were most concerned about the effects on the system of illegal and immoral practices in administration elites. Liberal critics of Mr. Nixon only found their old suspicions confirmed and had little new to say.

Those whose security depends immediately upon defense of the formal system expressed a variety of attitudes, most of them cautious. When the whole range of alternatives was being discussed—from forgetting about the Watergate affair, to living with it, through presidential resignation or censure or impeachment—they tended to have to find ways to excuse the President, as well as support the system, more readily than did intellectuals to both right and left.

However traumatic the effects of the scandals may be for years to come, they will probably not completely change the spiritual direction of America, which is not wholly set by the political climate. The morose and confused moods have begun to deepen and spread. But the exhausted political and religious left or moderates had not sufficiently regrouped or gained their second wind to lead in a new direction. Religious changes would have to tend to be self-generated in the immediate future, with less tone-setting from the White House.

However apt and accurate the angry protesters of the 1960s had been in their criticism of the formal system, they had not been able to project a believable positive alternative. In the larger society and in the religious sphere they suddenly disappeared almost without a trace and were hardly remembered. Their younger brothers and sisters first signaled the change with the handkerchiefs many of them whipped out when they sniffed through the bathos of *Love Story's* soap opera or clipped their way through the keepsake issues of *Life* magazine from the 1950s, when their parents were young.

Maybe "the movement" had never amounted to much. Vice-President Spiro T. Agnew always had blamed it on the media, whose cameras did tend to single out the most exotic or extravagant images of protest. Others had laid the fault at the feet of Dr. Benjamin J. Spock, the author of the baby book, and accused him of having sired a generation of children whose parents had been too permissive. Sociologist Peter Berger argued that a pampered generation had never known or envisaged suffering, poverty, disease, despair, or death. As it came of age in the face of the plotlessness of the Vietnam War and ghetto furies, some of its privileged and articulate spokesmen had to reach out for words and symbols to interpret life. They gave rise to a movement. Berger it was who also noted that people will call something a movement when a few thousand sons and daughters of academicians or mass communicators take up an old cause.

TECHNOPOLITAN UTOPIA

Actually, there had been three obsolescent "movements" in the 1960s. Three times, spokesmen came on the scene to show how the old, formal system would be forever totally transcended and how all citizens would be converted to a new one. In the early Kennedy years, at the beginning of the space age, the promised Utopia was technological. Man and society were becoming increasingly rational problem solvers. They were no longer haunted by spooks and ghosts. They had moved beyond meaning and myth and mysticism. Their natural future home would be in think tanks, at Hudson Institutes or Rand Corporations, in the offices of city planners, urban renewers, architects of technocracy. Together they would build a humane city. Those who looked backward or looked elsewhere, those who withheld consent from this imagery or did not fit its schemes, were described as victims of cultural lag. Eventually they would catch on and catch up.

MILITANT MESSIANISM

No sooner was this vision beginning to be outlined, grasped, and adhered to than did a second, more picturesque and threatening alternative arise. A kind of militant messianism was immediately understood by the larger society to represent "something worse." The war in Vietnam was not going well and the ghetto walls had not come down but the ghettos were burning. Justice had not prevailed. But, thought the majority, were the alternatives not worse? In their face, the advocates of "permanent revolution" offered their new way of life as an all-encompassing style. It drew on the dreams of people in developing nations, all of whom, it was prophesied, would soon experience wars of national liberation. It came from the rage of the poor and the ghetto dwellers.

The supporters of the formal system saw only the upheavals and threats: Dow Chemical recruiters besieged, deans locked up and the professors' files overturned on beleaguered campuses, "trashing," bombed research centers with scientists as victims, obscenities on walls, posters with pictures of Chairman Mao or Che Guevara supplanting American heroes. The larger public recognized that the revolutionaries were often more preoccupied with the success of their own movements than with the actual condition of the people they planned to help. How many movement people knew well even one black, one ghetto resident, one member of the Appalachian poor?

Four years later, whoever wanted to profit from discontent needed only to conjure up the slogans of "something worse" of the previous era. Recall of these served to unite the majority: "Join the Conspiracy." "Up Against the Wall." "Off the Pigs." "I Am the Americong." "Fuck the Draft." "Don't Trust Anyone Over Thirty." "Force Negotiation." "Welcome to Amerika." "W.I.T.C.H. Power." But the movements have come and gone. The Weathermen, S.D.S., Black Panthers, S.N.C.C., the Y.I.P., and the Crazies either disappeared or went straight and turned gentle, only to evoke less than mild curiosity.

The religious counterparts of these sensational evidences of permanent revolution had been less dramatic, but in some cases they outlasted the secular versions. James Forman publicized a "Black Manifesto" which asked for reparations from white churches. Months later, people yawned. Half-playful and slightly frantic causes like "Jonathan's Wake" and the "Yellow Submarine" barely outlasted, respectively, one-week conventions of the National Council of Churches or of the Presbyterian Church. The Roman Catholic left showed a bit more staying power. The priest-brothers Berrigan symbolized the most durable dissenting force, though by the time of the second Nixon inauguration, this Catholic left movement also had run into the worst kind of trouble. The public had begun to be bored.

THE MYSTICAL MILLENNIUM

Meanwhile a third alternative to the formal system was offered. Its rise overlapped the time of the permanent revolution's decline. The new choice was the more or less mystical millennium that almost went before it came by the name of the Age of Aquarius. This was Yale dreamer Charles Reich's "Greened America." He thought that it would inevitably overwhelm by the seductiveness of its gentility. It was "The Private Sea" that reporter William S. Braden described so accurately as he looked at gifted Americans who turned to the East or to drugs and mysticism for new sustenance. Theodore Roszak called it a "counter culture."

Suddenly many people stopped believing that the only style of consciousness that would ever again be permitted would be militant and violent. People tuned in, turned on, and dropped out. They followed the path of the guru of the year, drugsmith Timothy Leary, or pop mystic Alan Watts. The Maharishi Mahesh Yogi replaced media man Marshall McLuhan and the revolutionary shaman Herbert Marcuse, heroes of the two earlier-announced revolutions of sensibility. Norman O. Brown and R. D. Laing offered plausible psychoanalytic visions of alternatives to routine culture.

More welcomed because less threatening than was its predecessor, this Aquarian alternative has left more of a legacy than did the violent movements. An explicitly religious, although in few senses Christian, cause was being advocated, and it seemed more congenial. Religious hope began to come from the margins of society and not from the mainstream churches. The whole range of occult options was offered: metaphysics, astrology, scientology, ESP, voodoo, theosophy, Rosicrucianism, and a thousand cults. As R. D. Laing put it, people sought experiences that gave rise to theory and not theories of experience. They formed communes. Many of these cohered around religious rituals. Environmentalists called for a "rebirth of wonder," asking contemporaries to take a new look at earth and sky and air.

Anti-institutionalism was always a part of the mystics' program. Instead of turning down the sanctuaries, they simply ignored them. The call came: transcend, go above and go beyond organizations. Africa's primal vision was attractive to many: "Lift the stone and you will find me; cleave the wood and I am there." Leopold Sedar Senghor sang: "Why should I tear out my shrieking pagan senses?" The non-historical sense of Buddhism or the embracing vision of Hinduism mellowed grim Americans. Anthropologist Margaret Mead, no enemy of the young, first put her stamp on many of these ventures by proclaiming that salvation would come from the youth. Then she stepped back and regretted a scene of pathos: the young, she said, had had to form a mishmash of all the world's religions because their parents could transmit to them no living tradition.

The whole secular order was being wished away. Scientific explanations were unsatisfying, and approved symbols of reality were rejected. The larger public seemed to be of two minds about the trends. Certainly the drugs associated with this mysticism represented "something worse." Yet not all mystics took drugs. The communes were sometimes perceived to be un-American. But they were usually spatially remote and in few peoples' way. The long hair, beads, or saffron robes were puzzling or offensive visual images. But these were not basic threats, as the earlier, militant symbols had been. As twice before, a generation of prophets arose to announce that the new revolution would produce a new style of consciousness. All people except, for a time, the cultural laggard would inevitably adopt it.

Many of these almost forgotten or often past-prime movements were identified with youth. Were the youth really significantly different from their elders? All through the decade, some observers suggested that only a minority of young people had ever been involved. The Gallup and Harris polls time and again found only one or two percentage points of difference in the responses of young people on basic issues when contrasted with that of their elders. By the time eighteen-year-olds gained the vote and could exercise their rights in 1972, most did not bother to enjoy their franchise. Those who voted, fairly accurately mirrored their parents' world. Maybe there had never been more than a hint of revolution, expressed in exotic images.

The symbols, however, were effective in one respect. They drove the majority of people to reach for more ballast, to cling more tightly to nurse. During the year before the invasion of Cambodia and the deaths at Kent State, which turned out to represent the last gasp of the campus protest movement, Vice-President Agnew regularly conjured up images of exaggerated campus revolt for political purposes. Those close to the academic scene knew that basic change had come before the middle of spring 1970.

Peace had not arrived in Vietnam. The ghettos festered as before. Law and Order vied with Crime in the Streets, to agitate the public. The promises to which the three revolutions had addressed themselves had not come about, yet many people seemed glad simply to have survived the dissent. The self-indulgent young, when they gathered at the rock festivals or rejoined the straight culture, often acted as if they were glad they did not have to be as radical as their older brothers and sisters had been called to be. America seemed to have found an older, heavier balance and had "settled back."

NEW CONSCIOUSNESS

The most important revolutionary promises lay in the suggestion that a new consciousness was developing all along. Theologian John Cooper, seldom one to miss the opportunity to chronicle a vital cultural turn, announced the arrival of *The New Mentality* in 1969, just when the old one was actually beginning to reassert itself. The opening lines of his book reflected more the hopes of an era than accurate reporting. "A new form of consciousness is stirring within us . . . rising up from the unconscious depths, rising more ominously than ever before for things as-they-now-are. . . . The reactionary critics of the young and the young-in-spirit miss the whole issue if they see the new consciousness as only the older liberalism or the old radicalism of the left come into being in contemporary dress."

Instead, this new mentality, this "higher man" foreseen by philosopher Friedrich Nietzsche, represents "that event which so many natural scientists (as well as theologians) have declared impossible (or at least, not yet observed): an evolutionary transformation, a new step in the phylogenetic history of man." Three years later the old consciousness reasserted itself in the form of a huge majority voting for Richard M. Nixon. The crowds followed Billy Graham, conservative institutions sometimes prospered, and the old mentality prevailed. I happen to agree with Professor Cooper that a new consciousness or world view was and is developing, but it is less than a new "phylogenetic type." Nor is it developing at the pace and on the scale Cooper suggests.

CHANGES THERE ARE

The hidden drama implied in changing world views is important. Those who do not want to settle back with a comatose crew in a drifting societal ship try to discern its plot. There have been some changes in consciousness. However ambiguous some of the signs may be, they do offer hope to many. Reaction to the Vietnam War did not result in the birth of a newly moral or pacifistic nation. But the images of that conflict, brought to quiet living rooms at dinner hour, provided a bewildering picture of the military. They will almost certainly render more complex the prospect of future adventures of that type.

The changes in both self-image and the perception by others of blacks ("black power," "black is beautiful") has certainly produced a new complex of power and human identity in America. Not that racial justice has been secured. The political administrations of the 1970s know enough about the formal system to know that the white majority can be reduced to fear and exploited. But black personhood did become more visible, recognized, and feared or loved in new ways by the non-black majority. Ethnic consciousness has reappeared in a nation where the melting pot of immigrant peoples has not been successful at merging identities. Some of this ethnic assertiveness may be trivial and pointless. Over all, it has led to some sense of healthy variety and diversity in the formal system.

As a result of the latter two of the three revolutions of the 1960s a new ambiguity toward technology developed. Some reaction against utopian technology was silly. The world at large is not going to choose to reject technology. But it helped call into question the previously often unquestioned sway of the computer, and the computers-with-legs who run them and try thereby to determine peoples' destinies. The result was new opportunity by the public to ask how to achieve a more humane technological order.

Out of the ugly generational conflict of the 1960s came some surprising by-products, including the awareness that several generations coexist. Some of the young first worked with a two-generation theory: "Never trust anyone over thirty." They really were attacking the upholders of the formal system, the establishment of their parents' age group. As time passed, they often found new allies among the very aged. As they passed thirty themselves, they had to revise their views by developing some empathy for those who ran the society.

Few would claim that the sexual revolution has been an unmixed blessing, but there is at least less hypocrisy and more freedom for addressing the problems of human sexuality as a result of changes effected in the troubled sixties. As the bills for expenses come in, the ecological movement comes upon ever harder times. But it has made headway. Whereas in 1960 care of the earth, streams, or sky was still a program for a few outdoorsmen, visionaries, nuts, and hobbyists, by 1970 "consciousness raising" had occurred. The average man had begun to learn what was at stake in the efforts to reappreciate the environment.

The "soft revolution," in which people began to learn to come to terms with their bodies, may have led many to cultic self-devotion. At the same time, it liberated many people and often added to their experience of wholeness. Frequently communal experiments turned out to be short-lived, but they served to entice many in the larger society into considering options that they saw to be less suffocating than was the unextended family cooped up under one roof. Op and pop art or rock and electronic music enlarged the range of tolerance, which eye and ear accepted. Contact with Eastern and African religion similarly enlarged the scope of religious tolerance and led many to a new grasp of the spiritual realms.

Perhaps the longest-lasting revolution that reached the whole culture was the effort reborn in the 1960s to liberate women. To many men and women in the formal system, the movement's extravagances were threatening. They represented "something worse." The benefits were also so obvious that most people could never look back at "the feminine mystique" in the old way.

All the young were confronted by these changes at a crucial

stage of their development. Most non-whites and members of minorities learned of new opportunities. The leadership circles of women had found new images and instruments. Elites in the academy and the media were made newly aware of possibilities. Religious leaders could not escape the subtle influence of each of these widely advertised revolutions in consciousness. The 1960s, then, do not represent a dead loss, even though many legacies of the decade are being rejected, glossed over, or countered by new ballast in the 1970s. The changes do not represent a new human nature. They may or may not signify the presence of a new consciousness. But something having to do with an emerging new world view had been occurring.

WHEN CRISIS COMES

José Ortega y Gasset's picture applies to the generations formed in the 1960s: "A historical crisis exists when the modification of the world is such that the world, or the system of convictions of the preceding generation, is followed by a situation in which man is without the convictions, therefore without a 'world.' . . . In ages of crisis one finds frequently false and hypocritical opinions. Whole generations falsify themselves, that is, they escape into artificial styles, into doctrines, into insincere political movements, merely to fill the emptiness left behind by the genuine convictions."

On those terms the crisis did not end with the arrival of the generations of the 1970s, which in their frequently expressed taste for authority, fundamentalism, and simplism, also escape "to fill the emptiness." "The Age of Agnew" may have replaced "The Age of Aquarius," but hypocrisies remain. Observe the next salesmen's convention descending upon a city: the purportedly anti-permissive middle-class adult world patronizes the pornographic parlors. The adult of the straight culture argues his or her case against marijuana with blurry eyes and through the slurred speech induced by a third martini. The average man talks against violence but joins his President in making an obsession of football's violence, calls for Law and Order, or averts his gaze in the violence of the bombing of civilians.

The average man has found that the formal system has a safety harness. Hampden-Turner observed that "anomic men cling to the formal system, . . . to the fundamentalist religion and the 'certainty' of received truths." Such persons are acquiescent, moralistic, and chauvinistic. In each case, they reject the ambiguity of ideas and support the national, social, religious, or party structures instead. "Anomic man" related to *anomie*, which, in his book, refers to one's suffering from the sense that "everything is so uncertain," that he does not know "just how he is expected to act." Like novelist Georges Bernanos' character the "little priest," anomic man learns and then covers up the discovery that the night outside him terrifies him least: "God! I breathe, I inhale the night, the night is entering into me by some inconceivable, unimaginable gap in my soul. I, myself, am the night."

The battle between radical and anomic people seems to have quieted today, perhaps because the external symbols of the former have been largely repudiated or withdrawn. But in subtle ways the battles over world views and styles of consciousness continue, and the outcome is uncertain. In the 1970s, gains and losses are measured not by sizes of street demonstrations or numbers of votes. More important are the little signals: Who can still laugh or hope? How many compromises are exacted? Who can successfully care for the soul? Who remembers the persons involved in misery and not just one's own cause, movement, slogans, or vote?

Mood matters. Ortega observed: "Decisive historical changes do not come from great wars, terrible cataclysms, or ingenious inventions; it is enough that the heart of man incline its sensitive crown to one side or the other of the horizon, toward optimism or pessimism. . . ."

The radical caucuses at conventions of historians, scientists, or theologians in the 1970s were forlorn or deserted. The press paid lingering attention to each in the hope that something would happen in the midst of all-pervasive dullness. Tired old advocates reached for sensation one more time. The aging guru still makes occasional rounds of campuses, only to stare at night at the four walls of his motel room and to face the night in his soul. The leftover militant says a muffled "Boo," collects his dwindling lecture fee, and leaves the world as it was. The underground press lapses.

Must things remain this dull, this lifeless, this torpid? Must anomic man be abandoned to the leaders he chooses? Hampden-Turner had worried about both questions when he warned: "Where men fail to 'stand out' and renew themselves the culture is left only with dead things fashioned for earlier generations and now either discarded or manipulated for purposes never envisaged in their creation. Christ had a brilliant metaphor for the authorities of his time: 'Whited sepulchres, which indeed appear beautiful outward, but are within full of dead men's bones.'"

The 1970s, to almost everyone's surprise, found Americans continuing to discuss the place of religion in the world of anomic man. It will not come as a surprise, however, to note that American religion, adaptive as it so regularly is, has chiefly contributed ballast in this period of settling and stabilization. It has admirably begun to fill the injunction of Messrs. Streiker and Strober to give society what it wants. It is less profitable to mourn or whine than to ask questions about some possible future turns that can move a nation beyond the night in its collective soul, beyond the sepulchral scene that leadership has presented, toward a realm of human wholeness and hope.

2

That's Nice, Don't Fight

THE NEW AGENDA

The editors of encyclopedia yearbooks are paid to be alert to trends. The quality of their annual volumes depends in no small measure upon the success they have in locating the issues that drew the attention of the world during the year past. They daily read, clip, file, and sort stories chronicling the passing scene. In the course of the months they assign to various writers the task of summarizing the events they have noted in the fields of human endeavor.

Having written on religion in America in a number of these books for over ten years, I have had occasion to observe the great changes in what society perceives to be going on. The contrast between the world of the early 1960s and that of the early 1970s is startling. In the early 1960s the editors would regularly ask for comments on the ecumenical scene. Pope John XXIII was reigning. He had called for the convening of the Second Vatican Council. This event had alerted a larger public to a movement of Christian unity that had been growing in the Protestant and Orthodox worlds for a half century. What the churches were doing about their divisions made front-page news.

The other major area of curiosity had to do with the role of the churches in the public realm. President John F. Kennedy had been elected in the midst of one last controversy over whether a Roman Catholic should be the chief executive. Connections between religious and civil realms inspired public concern. Martin Luther King was coming to his prime. The presence of rabbis, priests, nuns, and ministers in his civil rights movement stirred many to reaction. What business was it of the churches to meddle in controversial affairs? This stirring made news, and the clerical participation made history. So the yearbooks duly and dutifully noticed the involvements.

Even the world of Christian thought was making news. At last, after centuries of foot-dragging, religious thinkers seemed to be coming to the point of finding ways to relate to a changing scientific and political world. The Jesuit scientist Pierre Teilhard de Chardin's evolutionary vision of a world whose very complexity was pointing to a fulfillment in Christ attracted notice. It signaled the extent of change within Roman Catholicism and stimulated responses among the Catholic faithful. Protestants Reinhold Niebuhr and Paul Tillich were aging. But a wider public had become aware of the ways in which they were dominating Protestant thought with ideas that often shocked the conventionally pious. Martin Buber's reflections in *I and Thou* led to a new Jewish formulation.

At the same time, a more radical kind of Protestant thought was being whispered about and eventually was to be bannered on the covers of newsweeklies. Some scholars argued that some historic symbols of faith were no longer applicable. Even the word "God" had become a problem. In the extreme case, some of the thinkers resurrected nineteenth-century atheist language and spoke of the death of God. According to *New Yorker* writer Ved Mehta, they wanted to make Christian thought very worldly, to square the circle, to make reason and faith at last "come out right." Their efforts could not but quicken public attention.

SPIRITUALITY SUPPRESSED

Christian unity, religious activism, radical thought: these made up the agenda of annual reports for some years. What was missing? No one thought to ask about the life of piety or spirituality. Almost all the predictors and projectors pictured all this to be waning, to mean less and less to people. Colorful religious movements at the fringes of society might perpetuate devotionalism. Prayer was, of course, a constant element in religious practice. But those who concentrated on such activities were supposed to be living on borrowed time. Could one "still" pray? Could one "still" expect the young to meditate? Could one "still" turn to world religion for signals of the spirit? The word "still" suggested either the uneasiness of the questioner—"I wish people could still do these things, but they can't"—or his sureness that they could not: the spiritual quest belonged to earlier stages of human history. Spirituality was being screened out as humanity moved toward its adulthood and past that adolescence in which it needed the crutches provided by the gods.

At mid-decade the American Academy of Arts and Sciences and the Church Society for College Work convened a conference on Religion in America at Boston. It gathered numbers of non-religious scholars of American life or Western history along with a comparable number of Jewish and Christian experts. The purpose was to bring together the various religious preoccupations and to produce an issue of the Academy's quarterly, *Daedalus,* and a subsequent book. The chapter titles of that book indicate something of the themes at mid-decade.

Best known was sociologist Robert N. Bellah's chapter on "Civil Religion in America." He showed how, when the churches failed to stimulate satisfying religious life, the society as a whole filled the vacuum. Historian Franklin H. Littell dealt with the churches and the body politic, discussing issues of church and state. Theologian Langdon Gilkey pointed to radical Christian thought and had to remind his readers that the spiritual motif was not yet wholly dead. Another sociologist, Thomas F. O'Dea, noted a crisis in contemporary religious consciousness, while a second theologian, Harvey G. Cox, isolated a "new breed" of cleric, the social activist. "These young activists are trying with some real success to lead the American churches away from their nostalgic dream of the rural past and into the peril and promise of an urban future."

Layman Daniel Callahan wrote on the Catholic counterpart in "The Quest for Social Relevance." Law professors Wilber G. Katz and Harold P. Southerland pondered religious pluralism and controversial Supreme Court cases, while another Catholic layman, Michael Novak, began to worry about whether some of the adjustments Christians were making meant a renewal or a slow abandonment of the faith. He argued that the preoccupying social involvement of the clergy was not a departure from Christianity but could be seen in a larger perspective as a contributor to its refreshment and re-creation.

Two Jewish thinkers did question some of the trends. Emil L. Fackenheim thought religion was becoming overexposed to the modern and secular world and was not drawing enough on its own resources. Milton Himmelfarb argued that some Christians' embrace of "secular society" was ill grounded and naïve. Historian William G. McLoughlin asked whether evangelistic and emotional sects and emphases at the edges of ordinary Protestantism would amount to much. He decided that the agitations associated with the name of Billy Graham did have continuities with the American religious past; they produced a degree of growth that was the envy of the historic churches, but they had probably crested with the rise and subsequent fall of their political favorite, Barry Goldwater. More significant was the fact that important religion in America was now pluralistic and not Protestant, and that Catholicism was undergoing a promising renewal.

A number of other scholars, whose work was not presented in the volume but who contributed to the two conferences, made a behind-the-scenes impact. Sociologists Talcott Parsons and David Riesman, editor T. George Harris, psychologist Henry Murray, and philosopher of history Frank Manuel all kept questioning the accents and projections of the churches' spokesmen. What *was* happening to the life of devotion and prayer, of piety and spirituality? Editor Stephen R. Graubard assigned me the task of accounting for it in an essay called "The Spirit's Holy Errand: The Search for a Spiritual Style in Secular America." Revisiting it now provides occasion for noting the climatic change.

"In the religious revival of the 1950's and the social revolution of the 1960's, formal, theological, and ethical obsessions crowded out spiritual concerns. In the process, *spirituality* as a term was abandoned, especially by academic religionists." During the 1950s the revival of religion had been organizational and programmatic. Newspapers had enlarged their religion sections in order to do justice to the stories of church building and rise in attendance. During the 1960s religion had become a front-page item because of its controversiality. "Urgent issues of theology, ethics, and the social forms of the church so preoccupied the elite and the avant-garde of the religious communities that they tended to ignore 'the spiritual dimension' of both individual and collective life."

Paul Tillich, America's most prestigious theologian in these decades, it was noted, had spoken of "the almost forbidden word 'spirit'" and had worked heroically to restore it to the vocabulary. "But even Tillich despaired of the attempt to resuscitate the adjective *spiritual;* it 'is lost beyond hope.'" But despite the lack of interest, and despite the despair of academic religionists, "concern for the spiritual did not, however, disappear. It went underground and became the property of adherents of America's folk, lay, civic, or societal religion. With or without formal leadership, a search for a spiritual style in America goes on."

What, then, were the evidences of a spiritual search at the heart of the religious quest? People kept on saying that they sought something of what Tillich called the "unity of power and meaning," which is denoted by the term *spirit.* Sociological surveys of Americans found most people believing in God and affiliating with church and synagogue. Only a few were interested in theology or ethical activism. "While religious institutions abdicate their roles in spiritual development as they face apparently more urgent concerns, the search becomes informal, and, one might say, para-religious." Best sellers then included the writings of Pope John, Dag Hammarskjöld, Teilhard de Chardin, and Malcolm Boyd in their devotional moments. People made Billy Graham, a devotionalist and enthusiast, a hero and criticized the Supreme Court for eliminating school prayer.

Meanwhile, typical religious leadership was often abandoning its interest in the meaning of the concept of "transcendence," of God beyond our strivings. The public was turning toward a kind of practical godlessness. Max Lerner was quoted as having said that, in the civil realm, "instead of finding their democratic faith in supernatural religion, Americans . . . tended to find their religious faith in various forms of belief about their own existence. . . . Resort to 'the spiritual' can serve as escape from responsibility into narcissism, from community concern into self-seeking. Thus John Dewey commented: 'What is termed spiritual culture has usually been futile, with something rotten about it.'" The essay lamented the general lack of leaders and guides in the informal and para-religious spiritual quests. "Despite all these complications, Americans are beginning to make their way with some creativity in their quest for a spiritual approach without a cosmic reference," whereas "traditional American spirituality would have found the question of transcendence, metaphysics, and cosmic order all-important."

THE SPIRITUAL TURN

This conference and its book-length reports demonstrate well the situation of the mid-1960s, one which seems to be the opposite of today's. The discussion of the spiritual was itself then marginal. It was an editor's afterthought and a writer's assignment—not his choice. The article is marked by a tone of apologetic and diffidence. A sort of shuffling of feet and clearing of the throat are evident: "How did I get hung with this topic that no one else wants to handle?" But the inquiries did turn up the suggestion that, from the new experiments, "a new language of the spirit could evolve. Today there are advocates of E.S.P., Psi-phenomena, and LSD. In search of spiritual expression, people speak in tongues, enter Trappist monasteries, build on Jungian archetypes, go to Southern California and join a cult, . . . see Jesus Christ as the man for others, . . . borrow from cosmic syntheses, and go to church."

So far as these churches, the traditional custodians of American spirituality, were concerned, "many responsible religious leaders are concerned [over] the spiritual barrenness of individuals and the lethal measure of the culture as a whole. Out of traditions, their resources, their partly disciplined community life, they were trying to speak words of judgment, of the future, of hope." It was hoped that renewed "spirituality would contribute to—but need not compete with—the deserving theological and ethical preoccupations of today's responsible Americans." It is not likely that such timid and modest words would have convinced yearbook editors in those years that they should devote much space to the devotional or emotional sides of religion.

By 1973 everything was different. One encyclopedia planned a four-part article on "The Great Awakening" of spirituality and asked for a piece describing the setting of revivals in the American past and present. Another proposed to deal with Pentecostalism, tongue-speaking, ecstatic experience, and healing—and solicited an entry on the history of such an emphasis in Christendom. Still another programmed a major piece on what had gone wrong with organized ecumenism, while an almanac's editors asked how the various Jesus and Spirit movements would relate to new organized evangelism efforts. No one asked about prosperous ecumenism, radical theology, social activism, or the public involvements of religious leaders, though some sort of story could have been concocted about each. The editors knew what the public would recognize as the current focus of power and meaning in religion.

Between that 1965 conference and the early 1970s the public had seen America coming apart, youth in what it regarded to be a dangerous tantrum, blacks burning cities, draft evaders leaving for Canada, religious leaders supporting "new morality" in sexual affairs, the military being scorned and the flag desecrated. The tolerance level for such activities never changed very much. In the spring of 1970, at the time of "Cambodia and Kent State," the polled citizens showed that they considered student revolt to be a vastly bigger social problem than the war itself or the racial situation.

THE SENSE OF RELIEF

When "the search for a spiritual style" in America resurfaced at about that time, it was generally greeted with a great sense of relief. The evangelical tradition that Professor William McLoughlin had thought would wane even if it survived after 1964 was prospering. The "underground" spiritual seekers of my essay had come up for air and basked in sunlight and under the glow of television camera lights. While many elements in the new revival would have been regarded as ominous or outrageous a decade earlier, one could almost hear a societal sigh of relief. Maybe the citizens' tolerance level had changed, and "straight" America could absorb shocks that would earlier have been disturbing.

The historic symbols of power and money are Caesar and Mammon. Caesar and Mammon had favored the religious revival of the 1950s, but naturally did not welcome the religious revolution of the 1960s. Both are visibly in approval of the spiritual strivings of the 1970s. The devotionalists, priests, enthusiasts, ecstatics, and healers get in no one's way and usually are supporters of the world of Caesar's and Mammon's making and liking. More important, the public that we described as adherents to the formal system welcomed the quieter agitations as opposed to the extravagances of the period of discontent and dissent.

A parable drawn from American folkloric humor illustrates the expanded degree of tolerance based on ignorance or a sense of relief. A slum mother on the upper floor of a tenement sends her contentious and noisy children outdoors to play in the alley below, just out of her view even when she steps out on the fire escape to draw a breath of summer's air. Relieved that they are out of her way but mildly puzzled by some sounds they are making as they engage in activities with neighbor children, she calls down, "What are you doing, children?" They answer: "We's f——, Mom." Her answer: "That's nice. Don't fight."

America in the first third of the 1970s was in a "that's nice, don't fight" mood. By contrast to what had gone on in the violent immediate past there were many occasions for relief. Harassed elders and others were ready now to tolerate almost anything that did not get in their own way. They had never welcomed the communes. But when these were in the hands of gentle Pentecostalists, they shrugged, "That's nice, don't fight." Respectable citizens would have stormed a drugstore newsstand a few years earlier had it been laden with books favoring witchcraft and Satanism, but they casually passed quietly patronized airport bookstalls that featured occult subjects with a post-Christian tinge. At least no barricades were up, no buildings were burning down, everything seemed harmless. "That's nice, don't fight."

Ten years earlier, square America had found rock music to be abrasive at best and demonic at worst. Long hair was a sign of anti-establishment protest and the short skirt signaled sexual freedom and the rejection of old standards. By the time of "Explo 72," eighty-five thousand moderately long-haired, moderately short-skirted youth gathered for a Jesus-centered, rock-beat rally in Dallas and everyone cheered. "That's nice, don't fight." At the very least, the new spiritualists ought to send the old dissenters some cards of thanks for the contribution the latter have made to an expanded consciousness, to a more lenient vision of experiment!

Any discussion of religious trends written halfway through the Nixon years has to focus on what the encyclopedia editors of 1962 forgot and those of 1973 remembered. The *Daedalus* authors had largely dismissed or noted only tangentially that an astonishing variety of expressions were available on the spiritual front. Religious emotionalism and ecstasy had supplanted both ecumenism in its formal style and activism in its clerical phase. The new agitations largely met the approval and the sponsorship of that very secular society that was never again supposed to care about metaphysics, meaning, myth, mystery, mysticism.

Whoever writes for those annuals or attends such conferences has learned or ought to have learned, of course, that nothing lasts: "This, too, will pass." Prediction is hazardous, but it would be foolish for anyone to believe that because people are speaking of a revival again it will be permanent. Nothing in the American past would lead an informed public to expect that ebb will not follow flow, decline follow rise, the trough follow the crest. Our very ability to put together the story of the awakening might be a sign that it has already passed its most creative stages of ferment. By the time it has become graspable, something vital probably has gone from it.

When the analysts were finally able, around 1958–60, to write on the meaning of the revival of the 1950s, that revival was disappearing "like cotton candy in the mouth of history" along with its benign high priest, President Eisenhower. By the time Protestant and Catholic thinkers had fashioned a "secular" theology to bring religion and the world into congruence and at the very moment when many of them were predicting that "religious man" would disappear with the dinosaurs of the past, religious man made a reappearance. When the general public noted his appearance and many cheered him in that "that's nice, don't fight" spirit, he may have begun to slip away again, to be reposed in the American Antique Shop along with the cool think-tank troglodytes of vintage 1960.

Religious man was back on stage early in the 1970s. And since he represents what may be some permanent elements in the human and cultural complex, he deserves attention. In the malaise of "the age of melancholy," when "the trend is trend-lessness," any sign of life would be noted with care. Those who are hopeful that "the promise of America" will always be in the process of being fulfilled and that the "promise of Christianity" will often find new embodiments would overlook the spiritual outbreaks to their peril.

What's going on? Is there a new "Great Awakening," as some analysts and partisans contend? Will there be a visible positive effect after the ferment has begun to be taken for granted?

SUPERNATURALISM AND SOUL

The spiritual movement went through several stages shortly after the turn of the decade. Without leaving behind or repudi-ating the previous phases, a new layer of experience was added each time. The movement has been from the secular to the reli-gious, sometimes from the religious to the Christian, and on oc-casion from the generally Christian to the specifically churchly. Not that a churchly stage is the only significant element on the scene. It is simply the most surprising new sign and should be seen in context.

Much has already been said about the secular motif, the suggestion that the human future would be non-religious and godless. It would belong, some prophets said, to people who had moved beyond the scope of traditional spiritual concerns. The summary of this future as provided by Herman Kahn when he looked toward *The Year* 2000, as recently as 1967, is a standard view. Depending in part upon social thinker Pitirim Sorokin, he and his computers set forth a "basic, surprise-free, long-term multifold trend." Culture and man would be "increasingly sen-sate (empirical, this-worldly, secular, humanistic, pragmatic, utilitarian, contractual, epicurean or hedonistic, and the like)."

This model was by no means replaced, but it had to share space with others in ways that Kahn could not easily have foreseen.

No dreary rehearsal of all the secular argument is necessary in the present review of a religious trend, but some recall of the general expectation as once announced is in order. The secular picture grew out of a belief that modern science, technology, politics, and ways of living would triumph. It gave ever more to man. Whatever seemed important to the human was man-made. The world was "rounded off unto itself." In 1965 Robert Boguslaw could still write of *The New Utopians* and mean the technicians and systems designers. Just as Alfred North Whitehead could once speak of the early-nineteenth century as the time "when wise men hoped," now Boguslaw summarized that period "when technical men hoped."

In religion, a pride of scholars urged in effect that Kahn's string of adjectives about the cultural and human future could apply also to Christian intentions. Christians not only should catch up with but should outpace those who were to bring in the liberating secular future. Zbigniew Brzezinski thought that "the largely humanistic-oriented, occasionally ideologically-minded intellectual-dissenter, who saw his role largely in terms of proffering social critiques" was rapidly being displaced "either by experts and specialists, who become involved in special governmental undertakings, or by the generalist-integrators, who become in effect the house-ideologues for those in power." As Boguslaw noted, "the new utopians . . . tend to deal with man only in his workaday world without prescribing . . . methods for achieving the good life. . . ."

Some Christian thinkers were effective at proving that Christianity had always had secularizing intentions. They agreed that it had always impelled man to dominate the environment.

(This, after Christians had been scolded for five hundred years for failing to assent to the secular tendency!) So successful were some apologists that a few years later environmentalists could suddenly attack Christians. Christianity had long helped demystify the world, and asked man to exploit nature through science and industry, it was said. Ironically, a five-hundred-year interpretation was suddenly forgotten, and a five-year-old one brought scorn on Christianity.

Life turned out to be not all governmental undertakings or powerhouse ideology. It was not even exhausted by workaday worlds. Too many people cared about spiritually "achieving the more abundant life" to permit the secular model to have a monopoly. If Kahn's, Boguslaw's, and Brzezinski's pictures applied to "operational" man, they spoke too little to passional man. Secularity remained and remains as an envelope around moderns. What to do, however, with that worldliness, still haunted people. Wonder, purged from the laboratory and legislature, reappeared outdoors or in bedrooms.

A national magazine startled me one autumn morning with its inquiry: Would I explore the idea of writing an article on "the new supernaturalism that is sweeping the churches"? What new supernaturalism? The answer was that Bishop James Pike had been talking to his dead son on "the other side." The bishop had become interested in the occult. A bit of research turned up the fact that Pike's Episcopal Church had either intentionally or accidentally ignored the whole matter. The religious press in general was undisturbed. A visit to a large magazine store revealed, however, that on cover after cover of the journals in the "Occult and Metaphysics" section, the late bishop's face was featured. I offered an alternative article on "The new supernaturalism that is sweeping the world and missing the church." The editors did not comprehend my assignment any more than I did theirs.

The editors of *Reader's Digest* like to invite visiting firemen to lunch at Pleasantville. "What's going on in religion?" was my question. My summary included the early-1960s version of ecumenism, activism, secularity. "What else is going on?" Then came the account of the new religious surfacings. One editor responded, "It seems as if the blacks, the kids, the women, the restless—all the exciting people—are doing religious things and talking about 'soul' while your church leadership talks about being organizational and worldly. Aren't you afraid that the two groups are going to pass each other in the aisle of the sanctuary, one going out while the other goes in?"

The best place to see the eclipse of the sun in 1970 was at Oaxaca, Mexico. The scientists and mass communicators were there; so were their college-age children. While parents filmed each other filming the eclipse, the young people were nearby munching on hallucinogenic "sacred" mushrooms or marveling at and with the natives who took their candles to church to ward off the spirits accompanying the darkness at noon.

TOWARD THE SANCTUARY

The Christian thinkers who had been telling us to embrace the secular took a second look and began to write about celebration and the rebirth of wonder. But this celebration and wonder were noted largely, at first, outside the orbit of religious institutions. Much of it had ominous overtones which frightened conventional churchgoers.

A new, more acceptable stage arrived with the announcement of "the Jesus movement" in its freakier stage and "the Pentecostal movement," as spirit-filled worship began to make its way into the respectable churches, however much it remained at their margins. A few hundred West Coast young people pushed a few score others into the Pacific, baptized and embraced them, made beautiful pictures for *Look* and *Life,* and a "movement" was born. While extravagant and extreme at first, the movement turned ever more straight as the culture did the same, and most members conformed almost instantly to the new Nixonian mood.

By the winter of 1970 they were ready for the sanctuary. I recall an evening at a prominent church in Berkeley when a dozen of them asked for "equal time" after a lecture on religious trends. The rabbi's son, the black, the Chicano, the Ph.D. in chemistry, the ex-drug addict, and other typical exotics all took their measured place on stage and in measured pace presented simple if rather repetitive witness. What impressed me most was the curiosity and tolerance of the audience, which was made up chiefly of alumni of Bay Area Protestant seminaries and their spouses, back for annual retreat and nurture.

Few in that audience would have agreed with the simplistic theology they were hearing from the witnesses. Almost none would have been happy to have an outbreak of "freakism"—which was then supposed to be breaking out like a contagious disease—in their own parishes. But the audience was respectful and attentive; relief was visible on their faces. My God! this, after all, was Berkeley! And these were nice young people who were not shouting obscenities, or smoking pot, or storming the campus, or trashing. They may have been unconventionally and disturbingly overreligious as their older siblings had once been oversecular. But, all in all, their act was reassuring. "That's nice, don't fight."

A year or two later, the fervent began to find a new home

in the sanctuary. The churches have since set out to domesticate the enthusiasm and to generate some of their own. The modes of spirituality grasped from the contacts with Eastern religion, African wonder, Western occultism made their impact. These will not simply be repudiated; that airport bookstall should remain in business for a long time. But Westerners are not all going to "jump out of their skins and out of their culture." They became involved with a homecoming. The African Bantu had a saying: "He who never travels thinks mother is the only cook." Media, travel, college classrooms, mobility—all these had made it possible for a generation to "travel" spiritually, to pick and choose religious options. This restless and gifted edge of the Jesus-Pentecostal freakism began to re-explore the more conventional pieties of their own tradition.

Meanwhile, taking advantage of the climatic change and drawing on their own overlooked resources, the more straight and square churches, far from the Berkeleys and the communes, got themselves together for new ventures in devotionalism. The long-out-of-vogue "marginal" churches often attracted more attention than did the conventional and generally visible ones.

Strange, is it not, to speak once again in churchly and even denominational terms about the spiritual search in secular America? There is a great danger, of course, that one can become too "churchy," simply out of a sense of surprise. Too many distractions and competitors remain for any thoughtful person to be swept away by ecclesiastical propaganda. The uncritical musings about freaks and Pentecostals by off-guard and awed mass communicators should count for little. A new triumphal note in reporting on the churches would be foolish. But with all fingers crossed and bets hedged, with all defenses against gullibility up and all senses alert, it is still possible for a reporter to list revival in the churches among the noteworthy cultural phenomena present in the early 1970s.

THE AMERICAN EXCEPTION

Sociologist Thomas Luckmann provides one of the better schemes for noticing where religion goes (or went) in the modern world. He speaks of *The Invisible Religion* because most of it "went" out of the church and synagogue. Luckmann, too, does not believe that man and culture are or can soon become simply worldly, simply secular. The question is, how will they come to terms with meaning and belonging? In his widely accepted picture, the modern world does not allow for the state to coerce people to accept a faith. A culture will not ordinarily be homogeneous enough that everyone in it can accept a single unifying philosophy. Religion tends to become a private matter. People hack out little momentary circles of belonging. Eight people who are "into" astrology get together. Some Zen addicts or Jesus freaks find each other and form a huddle. People are religious on their own, in response to private reading or their personal thoughts.

Not everything is private, however. Much religious activity goes on in a "sacred cosmos" that is not under the custodianship of the priest or minister. The nation may provide religious meaning for many people. "Church-oriented religion is on the periphery of modern society." This kind of situation is more obvious in Europe than in America. The more rural an area was in Europe, the more likely it was still to be "religious." The world is becoming a city. In the older findings, women practiced religion more than did men, but as women are liberated from domestic roles this circumstance is changing. Middle classes are more church-related than are members of the working class. In Europe only a small minority was interested in church life beyond the rituals of baptizing, marrying, burying, and the like.

In America, matters were somewhat different until around 1960, when the lines on the graphs of growth at last leveled and in some items declined. Luckmann was not sure what to make of this fact. "Caution is indicated in summary characterizations of church religion in America." There has here been no feudal past or peasantry. The frontier experience brought a different kind of church activity. Immigration and ethnicity helped people affirm their religious traditions. Sudden urban and industrial change had been faced in ingenious ways. The presence of blacks and the early spread of the middle class made room for distinctive styles of religiosity. Puritanism, separation of church and state, revivalism, sectarianism—all these gave America a unique history and an astonishing array of options.

Luckmann concluded that with "one exception—the relatively high involvement of Americans in church religion—" most Western nations invite the conclusion that church-oriented religions have become marginal. American churches are also now more and more pervaded with secularity, and the church has been relocated in society. People bring different expectations from formerly. For instance, in contrast to the longer past, clienteles generally do not want churches to take responsibility for political, social, economic, and other public affairs. That would be "meddling." They are to content themselves with being boxed in, confined to dealing with private, familial, and leisure spheres. Even these are being crowded by secular competitors and measured by non-religious norms. What will the high-rise apartment, the general disappearance of the single-family home, and the extension of the weekend do to church religion, revived or not? This is, in effect, what Luckmann has asked. He also suggested that even churchgoers do not get all their religious signals from their local priest and congregation.

People informed by such an analysis could charge that we are talking about teapot tempests and big fish in little ponds, then, when we talk at all about revivals that touch the churches and synagogues. But these do remain the main custodians of religion in the society. One hundred million people take pains to be somehow identified with them. Their historic roots are deep. They may not have what Trotsky called "the privilege of historical backwardness." Therefore they cannot leapfrog over many stages of tradition, as the Yippies, trashers, or revolutionaries did in order to get attention. But in a thousand ways they quietly impose themselves on national consciousness and deserve attention.

THE ACCENT ON EXPERIENCE

The first element to notice in the spiritual recovery is the dimension of experience. Everyone wants to have a religious experience, and not merely be told about it. God is to be "addressed, not expressed," said Buber. This hunger was restored to many after they had visited spiritual kitchens other than mother's. A clerical friend of mine reports on an afternoon several summers ago: Two "hippie-looking young men" presented themselves at his midwestern church and asked whether they could use it. The pastor was an advocate of the free use of churches for whatever causes concerned people. But he had known numerous occasions when people who had used the building in support of controversial causes then identified his congregation with these causes. So he had gotten into the habit of asking why people wanted to use the edifice, as a matter of information for his next day's task of public relations to some of his congregation.

"We'd like to meditate. We are thumbing out to Berkeley later on, and thought we'd like to contemplate for a few hours." His first impulse, he confessed, was to think: "What are you, a couple of nuts? Whoever heard of using a church for meditating?" His second thought: this church has a sign in front saying that it is open all daylight hours for prayer and meditation. No one had ever bothered to use it that way apart from the time of worship by the whole assembly. Third thought: the black books on the minister's shelves more often urged people to have leisure and know that God was God or taste and see that the Lord was good or to meditate on His ways than they enjoined people to become world-beaters. "Go ahead!"

Western religious resources for experience and meditation are rich. Western people simply allowed their personal interests in them to atrophy. The visits to the East and to Africa were often the first steps for spiritually mobile white Westerners to undertake, if they wished, to find their own roots. They began to ask basic questions again about what it meant to be religious.

The Hasidic tale that prefaces this book illustrates the new way of posing the question. The first-generation rabbi lit a fire at a place in the woods, said a prayer, and all was well. His successor said, "The fire we can no longer light, but we can still say the prayer." A deadening process of retreat from experience had begun. The third generation neither lit the fire nor knew the prayer, and the fourth could do no more than tell the story. We might add, as some playful or mournful commentators have done, that today we do not even tell the story for its own sake. We examine its status as a legendary tale, or see how it illustrates Jewish piety.

In America in the 1970s, a significant number of people are going back, for a variety of reasons, to that fatal turn taken in second-generation religious experience. In that generation the rabbi said, "The fire we can no longer light." They ask: "Who says so?" And they answer, out of passing fancy or deep conviction:

"The fire we can light."

Such an affirmation or expression of hope will mean many things to different persons or groups. This book is designed to explore some claims and efforts.

The new spiritualizers would say that the great Maggid betrayed them when he said, "The fire we can no longer light, but we can still say the prayer." *Why* could the fire not be relit? What cosmic event had made experience impossible? Why should believers be told that once upon a time there were prophets and mystics, visionaries and ecstatics—but that now all potentials for a revisiting of their kind of experience has disappeared? Why should the churches recall the story but not re-enact it? Why should people content themselves with words about experience instead of having the experience itself?

The early attempts at fire lighting were often received with less favor than were later versions. There were reasons for fear. Herman Kahn, again following Sorokin, had envisioned that after the present late sensate or secular culture a new stage in history could come. It is characterized as underworldly, expressing protest or revolt, overripe, extreme, sensation-seeking, titillating, depraved, faddish, violently novel, exhibitionistic, debased, vulgar, ugly, debunking, nihilistic, pornographic, sarcastic or sadistic. That almost sounds like middle America's newspaper accounts of both the militant and mystical stages of what used to be called the counter culture. The "that's nice, don't fight" stage had not yet appeared. Caesar, Mammon, and parents could not yet smile, nor could the formal system integrate these erratic efforts into itself.

THE NEW MOVEMENTS

The first signals in the Christian orbit were associated with what came to be called the Jesus and the Pentecostal movements. Their separation eventually could continue in their extreme forms at the margins of society, subjects of media curiosity but not choices for many. The "Children of God," a communal sect that made much of a couple of biblical passages that ask children to leave their parents, represented this first option. Or they could become new denominations. Like many earlier protest movements in the American past, they began anti-denominationally. Before long, some of them began to look and sound like denominations and to drift into the patterns they had set out to repudiate. Possibly one or another of the youth-minded organizations may someday find it difficult to work with existing churches and may thus form one of their own. Notoriously difficult as it is to inaugurate a full-scale denomination these days, we should not expect much of this trend. As a third direction, these movements may quietly begin to feed into the existing churches. These provide a shelter or umbrella for many kinds of influences, and are artists at co-option. The trend toward such absorption and influence is already evident.

The rise of the various experience-centered forces occurred during a late stage of the "counter culture." The campuses, those arenas beloved by the media and frightening to the American majority, had begun to turn quiet. Most public notice in the world of religious experiment turned toward the overadvertised "occult explosion." At that time, Father Andrew Greeley, alert to the campus picture, wrote an article in which he observed that far from being secular and merely worldly, the spiritually mobile element among the youth were devoted to every kind of magic, superstition, religion, or cult ever known to man. One could respectably participate in all of these. No, there was one exception: one could not be devoted to classic Christian piety or to fundamentalism. But the circumstance Greeley described could hardly be expected to prevail in a culture that contained such a strong Christian reminiscence.

My awakening to the cultural ferment over religious experience before the churches began to domesticate it, occurred not long after I had made a chance remark on Canadian television. The remark came close to what Greeley had said: "Give me a weekend in Toronto alone and I could find groups expressing every form of magic or superstition ever known to man." People challenged both the station and me to make good on such a statement. By autumn of 1970 I had spent three weekends in Toronto following up on nineteen script suggestions: "Find me a witch, a Satan-worshipper, a hare krishna group, a sorcerer or soothsayer, a Hindu, a Buddhist, and the like." With little difficulty the researchers found all of them in Toronto except a haruspex. The haruspex does what some old Roman priests did. They predicted the future by gazing at animal entrails when the animals were being sacrificed. They tell me one could have been imported from Los Angeles, but that would have been cheating.

The television producers filmed all the exotics and new-style religionists in action, while Christian prayer and mysticism were only talked about. It was felt that portrayals of these would not awaken much public curiosity. Not many months later, however, the colorful California members of the Jesus movement were attracting the camera's eye.

JESUS AND THE SPIRIT

No one knows quite what the "Jesus movement" is, or was, or how many people are or have been part of it. A kind of revolving-door effect is at work in these movements. It is hard to know on what the movement has been building or what it has been displacing. As so often before, the society at large convinced itself that there was a "Jesus revival." Visible groups certified the conviction. Soon a bandwagon effect was operative: "Be the first kid on your block to join the Jesus movement." The excitement offered color in a gray decade, was exotic in a bland season, presented a lively alternative to campus revolt or high school apathy. Here was an outlet for spiritual energies, and a means of dissenting against something—in this case, against rigid institutional religion—while also providing people with a means of finding new ways to affirm the past.

Most important, the turn to Jesus offered people some possibility for having a religious experience in a traditional and developing cultural context. Turning to Jesus was like turning the pages of an old family album. The revival lore in America is so deep that a new generation could still fall back on it. The public met the movement with considerable tolerance. After a sight of the extravagant communal forms such as the "Children of God," parents were happier than ever that their children were finding moderate ways to "groove with Jesus." "That's nice, don't fight." The conservative churches, many of them once far removed in thought patterns and personal styles from those of the Jesus people, were surprisingly tolerant of them.

Religious experience (as opposed to, say, social activism or theological interpretation) has been a frequently championed feature in American history. Never has there been a religious renewal that was not somehow born in emotion and tinged with enthusiasm and ecstasy. The First and Second Great Awakenings in the 1730s and early 1820s relied on what Perry Miller called "the rhetoric of sensation." They fostered sawdust trails and anxious benches, "jerks" and swooning, altar call and soul songs, gatherings at the river and mass rallies. The more recent revivals followed similar patterns. Historic precedents could perhaps be violated in the future. Maybe new styles of consciousness are emerging and emotional or personal experience will be downplayed. But the fact that precedent was being followed in the 1970s gave many a sense of confidence that America was once again back on target and renewal was on schedule.

The early Jesus movement turned out to be the domesticated and acceptable version of the counter culture. For Jews, the revival of Hasidism, which is a kind of ecstatic and joyous Jewish mysticism, served in a similar role. Many Roman Catholics experienced a movement of the Spirit which was often called Catholic Pentecostalism. Each of these picked up an authentic strand of tradition and enlarged or exaggerated it. Thus H. Richard Niebuhr has noted that historic American Protestantism often looked like "a Unitarianism of the Second Person of the Trinity," which theologically precise types would have no difficulty finding to be a chief characteristic in much of the expression of the early Jesus people. They were not looking for definitions but for immediacy.

By itself, enthusiasm is not long sustained. Sparks die, fires become embers, flows ebb, lava crystallizes, ferment wanes. Second generations have more difficulty with lighting spiritual fire. Thus the new Pentecostalism in Catholic, Episcopal, Presbyterian, and similar churches attracted notice around 1960. It began to be a campus reality around 1968–69. Before long, huge conferences of Pentecostals gathered each summer on the

Notre Dame campus. Almost instantly, the unorganizable began to be organized. Similarly, in the Jesus circles, Campus Crusade, Young Life, and denominational "Youth Encounter" movements soon captured the energies and channeled them into thoroughly respectable passageways to the larger society.

Once such turns occurred, these movements stood some chance of outlasting most other, come-and-go experiences and immediacies. They bore enough similarity to elements in existing church life that they could trade on people's sense of reliance on the familiar. There had always been "Jesus people" in Protestantism, but the real ecstatics had usually been isolated or rural in their origins. Now once again middle-class America borrowed or rediscovered "soul," or stumbled into coincidence with versions of it that had been the property of urban lower classes. For seventy years there had been formal Pentecostal denominations or groups in American religion. These had usually been denominationalized in largely lower-middle-class groups. But now once again middle-class America could spiritually "go slumming" and trade on some of the experience of simple, fervent tongue-speakers.

The question of transmittability of the new fervor preoccupied many. Rural-based pietism could be passed on through many generations, in numerous social classes. Fundamentalism had found its routes for transmission. But ecstatic religion in which a person literally "stands outside one's self" has not often or long been able to be passed on. Either the adherents move up in social class and out of the contexts in which the vision first came to them, or their children change cultural contexts and cannot hold on to the old fervency in the new settings.

Almost as if by instinct, those who favored the movements of spiritual experience seemed to sense that these would best survive if they lived off existing churches or fed into them. As a result of these and similar religious outbreaks, the denominational configuration and accents in America began to change. The future shape of organized religious life in the nation may be considerably different as a result of stirrings that came late in the 1960s.

Before attempts to anticipate this shape, to understand the alternatives, or to make decisions about the value of various options can be effectively undertaken, it is necessary to try to discern why recent pressures lead people to drastically opposed styles of response. In the same world, one set of people seems to be open to everything and to lose their identity, while another set prematurely closes itself off. The story of these expansive and constrictive styles is at the center of the American religious drama today.

3

Open and Shut Cases

THE EXPANSIVE OR OPEN STYLE

Tomorrow's religion and tomorrow's Christianity in America will be both more expansive *and* more constrictive, more pluralist and more sectarian, more sprawling and more rigidly defined. This will be the case because the population that is seeking religious answers is itself divided about the opposing and contradictory tendencies.

To introduce expansive religion ("dilatable, spreading, taking in many things, having a wide range"), let me introduce an almost archetypical young American. Naturally, the encounter took place on an airplane, where most personal illustrations in the religious world seem to originate. Naturally, the representative of what I shall call a Protean way of life was a Californian, who is therefore more typical than anyone else. This young person was a flying example of the boundarylessness that characterizes so much modern psychic and spiritual experience.

While returning from the huge Congress of Learned Societies in the Field of Religion which had met at Los Angeles in September of 1972, I was reading a book on science and the Christian faith. This endeavor was induced by a sense of panic, because two days later I was to read a paper giving a historian's interpretation of this subject, about which I knew so little. After a nap during lunch, the California seatmate spotted the title on the seat between us, and a conversation began.

"Are you a Christian?" Yes, I supposed I was. "Are you a Jesus person?" Of course; forty-three years earlier I supposed I had become one of them. "And do you like science?" How does one like or not like science? I was ignorant, but interested in it. My time for questioning her eventually came.

A twenty-one-year-old coed at a junior college in Los Angeles, she was celebrating her birthday by spending part of a medium-sized inheritance on a visit to a grandmother in New Jersey. She had moved from that state at age three. She was attracted to the book title on the seat next to her because she wanted to be a scientist. The coed was a member, she said, of the Jesus movement. She liked science because she wanted to be of some worth in the world, and liked Jesus because of the virgin birth, physical resurrection, and Second Coming. Her parents were a Jewish-Gentile agnostic couple ("probably atheistic, if they thought about it") who had not understood her conversion. They had gone along enough to let her switch recently to a Jungian, and hence, she said, a psychoanalyst more religious than her previous one had been.

She was "into" Zen Buddhism and yoga, but the Jesus people had reached her and brought her to the Church of Christ. I intervened: "Church of Christ; that's fundamentalist, isn't it? Tell me about your minister; what's he all about?" Her answer: "Well, this Church of Christ is a little different. I have two ministers, and they are not he's, they are she's. And we have seances and things." When she later learned that I had been back recently to my childhood home after many years and remembered events from the time when I was three, she allowed that she also remembered her New Jersey childhood, which ended at age three. "Don't the psychologists say we can't really remember back that far in our lives?" "Oh," she said, "you and I are different. I can tell from talking to you that you entered your current body all charged up, the way I did, from a previous life that was probably cut off early." Reincarnation. Before the flight was over, I learned that she believed that she could fly without flying, through astral projection.

PROTEAN MAN

Admittedly, one may not find too many boundaryless people like this down the block in the nearest fundamentalist church. But her psychic layering, her ability to absorb so many layers of experience, is widespread. Aristotle's law of contradiction had little meaning to her. My coed friend could see no reason why she might have to choose between concepts of resurrection and reincarnation, between Eastern and Western views of history and its purpose. They were equally available and all addressed to her.

Robert Jay Lifton's "Protean man" came to mind as the model. Such a personality does not possess a relatively fixed character. Self-process given to flow and fluidity dominates. Such people have been flooded by imagery, particularly because of mass communications. Everything in the world seems accessible. Nothing is ruled out. No tradition can be appraised in isolation from others. Here is where Margaret Mead's comment about "mishmash religion" is a propos.

Mike Royko, columnist extraordinary, once fantasized a visit by a young person who, it occurred to the columnist, had encountered him before in various movements of the decade. As I recall the sequence in broad outline, the aging youth had already been the organization-man student, the angry trashing militant, the drug-obsessed Eastern mystic. Now he was a Jesus person. Royko in effect breathed a sigh of relief for his guest. At last he had found a permanent center for ordering his life. Well, maybe, said the visitor. Still, averred the Jesus-movement spokesman, he thought he might yet want to be a cowboy when he grew up.

These persons' ability to add layer upon layer of experience and imagery onto their spiritual grasp can be compared to a palimpsest. The palimpsest was a parchment that could be scrubbed clean or erased repeatedly like a slate, and ever a new layer of writing be imposed. But the older levels never completely disappeared. Experts could trace several earlier layers under the more recent additions. The modern psyche similarly often has to undergo a kind of psychic layering. For a person to become a Christian could represent the rejection, erasing, or at least partial forgetting and blockage of other and earlier signals and symbols. But there is a difference between the act of turning now, and the isolation of Christian choice in the past.

Grandfather could be unreflectively traditional. He did not have to acquire a tradition, the way sociologist Will Herberg's confused third-generation heir of immigrants reached back for the Catholic religion of the Italians as they were losing their language and their lore. He would not have been able to reach back to Africa for sustenance if he were a slave on a plantation, as his college-bred descendants can do. He did not need to decide *whether* to express his ethnicity. No language but that of his own foreign-language group was available for him to express himself at all. Spiritually, East and West never met for him, and religious signals seldom reached him from outside his own ghetto, his ward, his valley. His world had boundaries and he knew them.

The act of accepting or rejecting the symbols of a faith from within a tradition is different from entertaining and embracing them in a cafeteria line of options. When the student of counter culture, Theodore Roszak, asked people to act *as if* the world were magical, he was invoking a different response from the one people made back when it would not have occurred to any of them that the world might not be magical. When theologian Harvey Cox, in the *Feast of Fools,* asked people to treat the world as if it were enchanted, and to return to a mythic sense of creation, he called for something different from what would have come forth from people who really knew it was enchanted, had never heard the word myth, and did not know that one could choose elements of a world view.

Expansive religion or Christianity has assets that compensate in part for the psychological blurring. Some people have re-learned their own roots and possibilities as a result of having traveled and visited spiritually. They have learned to meditate after visiting the East, and to dance after becoming aware of Africa. Catholic Christianity sometimes calls for a kind of boundarylessness, for openness to competing and jarring signals and sounds. But unless a person has a principle or philosophy for some sort of coherence, boundarylessness can lead to dilettantism and the loss of depth at best or disintegration at worst. Fearing such disintegration, some people reach for the polar alternative to the Protean, or expansive, style.

CONSTRICTION: SHUT CASES

A newly constrictive religiosity is appearing on the scene at the same time, often among and even within the same people. Our culture manifests contradictory tendencies, and people who wish to project the future have to be able to comprehend both. If they are successful, they can congratulate themselves by recalling F. Scott Fitzgerald's observation that "the test of a first rate intelligence is the ability to hold two opposed ideas in the mind at the same time, and still retain the ability to function."

Robert Jay Lifton noted the psychological alternative to his Protean man when he spoke of a concurrent cultural tendency "which seems to be precisely the opposite of the Protean style." He elaborated, "I refer here to the closing off of identity, the constriction of self-process, to a straight-and-narrow specialization in psychological as well as in intellectual life, and to reluctance to let in any extraneous influence." Lifton sees this as being chiefly a one-dimensional reaction, a psychological backlash. The constrictive pattern differs from the earlier styles which had grown out of society and tradition; "the constricted self-process . . . requires continuous psychological work to fend off Protean influences which are always abroad."

In Lifton's light we can see, for example, essentially two Jesus movements, two Pentecostalisms. The older one lives on in continuity with existing society or tradition and experiences inner renewal from time to time. Rural Southern Baptists never stopped being Jesus people. If they suddenly become assertive and grow from time to time, they do this with little inner strain and with considerable possibility that they can transmit their character and style to another, succeeding generation. Members of longer-term Holiness or Pentecostal churches can also at least make efforts to perpetuate their long-held gifts of the Spirit. They do not need the often frantic sense that the newer Pentecostalists often seem to have to demonstrate.

The second set of enthusiasms is the product of Protean, expansive America with its media and their options, its pluralism and the attractions that go with it. The phrase "to be 'into'" something characterizes this second style. People are "into" Jesus, or they are "into" Pentecostalism. The word suggests that they have previously been "into" something else and are headed for something else, so they have to pursue their current option with special intensity while they screen out all other signals. This "constricted self-process" in the individual or group exacts constant efforts for people "to fend off Protean influences." It is one thing for Jesus people in Berkeley to be fanatic about Jesus as "The One Way" and another thing for citizens of a southern city, where everyone is Baptist, Methodist, or members of the Church of Christ.

A NEW POWER COMPLEX

Taken together, both the strenuous and the more casual fending off of Protean influences on the part of millions of Americans had led to a new complex of power in the denominations by the early 1970s. It represented the conservatives' half of the inning. The media and the public had given due attention to the ecumenists, social activists, and radical thinkers in the 1960s. After 1968, under a different leadership in Washington, a new spiritual style won favor, while the churches that had so often profited from the revival of the 1950s and endured the revolution of the 1960s languished.

Actually, the newer boomers had never been so far out of contention as their advocates later pictured them to have been. All during the fifties and sixties Americans were reminded that the majority of Protestants and Catholics made up a rather traditionalist and near-fundamentalist body, even if the smaller and more experimental or more exposed churches were getting attention. Those who are obsessed with boasting about growth always have to show how small they were *before* their spurt, and have to exaggerate the size and power of the groups they are displacing in the public eye. Still, on a percentage basis the trend was unmistakable.

TWO DENOMINATIONAL FATES

No broadly acceptable typology of the two sets of denominations has emerged. A picture that often helps me to do some sorting grows from my childhood geography book. It printed a topographical map of the United States on which were two sets of mountains. The one set was colored gray to represent "old, worn-down" mountains. In the West were jagged, brown-colored peaks. The legend told us these were "young, rugged mountains." While the case of Roman Catholicism is somewhat different, for reasons that derive from world-wide change in that church, in Protestantism the "old, worn-down" denominations are wearing further down, while the "young, rugged" denominations are being pushed up higher and are offering an ever more jagged and prominent skyline.

A glance at American history and the map of denominations provides significant clues. In colonial America there were basically three and a half Protestant denominations of statistical note that survive in contention today. The President of Yale College, Ezra Stiles, in 1783 plausibly prophesied that the American future would be about equally divided between these Congregationalists, Presbyterians, and Episcopalians. The "half" refers to a wing of separating Congregationalists then on the scene. It came to be the heart of the northern Baptist church groups. Roman Catholicism and Judaism were barely represented, and the foreign-language-speaking Mennonites, Anabaptists, Lutherans, and Reformed of the middle colonies did not seem to fit in and could not dream of running the show.

Between 1940 and 1970, according to the *Yearbook of the American Churches*, the American Baptist Convention, heirs of those dissenters against Congregationalism, declined by 5 per cent. (The Southern Baptist Convention profited from late-nineteenth-century revivals as its northern counterpart did not, and henceforth has a virtually entirely separate history.) The Congregationalists, now joined by a Reformed and once-Continental group to form the United Church of Christ, had grown by 15 per cent. The mainly northern United Presbyterian Church in the U.S.A. enlarged by 33 per cent and the more southern Presbyterian Church in the U.S. by 80 per cent. The third on Stiles' screen, the Episcopal Church, had grown by 65 per cent. Except in the case of the American Baptist Convention, all this sounds impressive—until we recognize that the population of the nation had grown by 58 per cent. Therefore, only the Episcopal Church and the largely southern Presbyterian body experienced a net gain. These are the heirs of colonial American citizens, and they form five of the six slowest-to-grow (or declining) denominations in recent decades. The United Methodist Church, formed a year after Stiles spoke, is the other relative decliner, having grown by only 33 per cent, while in the nineteenth century it had expanded most impressively.

OLD DOMINION DENOMINATIONS

Americans should think of these as the "old dominion" denominations, since they originally took responsibility for relating religion positively to the culture. They were—except for those Baptists—largely established, and they became the establishment. Largely white, they projected WASP values and took over the custodianship of the evangelical empire. They were necessarily most exposed to the environment, least protected by "constrictive" possibilities, most open to theological pluralism, most secularized by long erosive tendencies.

These "old dominion" groups had long before seen their dominion begin to disappear as they were being progressively disestablished by Catholics, Jews, the unaffiliated, Continental Protestants, and newer sects. Significantly, most of these do not show up as groups that mastered or dominated any territories on today's religious atlas. A map of "Religion in America: 1950" colors solidly "the denomination that accounts for at least 50% of the reported religious membership in the county," or shows a striped color when a denomination accounts for over 25 per cent but less than 50 per cent of that membership.

Where do the "old dominion" churches dominate? One county each in the western parts of Nebraska, Wyoming, and Colorado—hardly population centers—have a United Church of Christ membership majority. Unitarianism was an early branch off colonial Congregationalism. There is one Unitarian majority county, in western North Dakota. The Episcopal Church has a majority in seven equally underpopulated counties in South Dakota and the other three states just mentioned. This is hardly a bastion. One county in western Colorado and one in northern Nebraska are the only two American Baptist Convention strongholds. The eye catches only two northern (Colorado) and one southern (North Carolina) counties where Presbyterians hold majority positions. Very few counties are "striped" with designations for denominations that held colonial and early-national positions of dominion. These remain sizable church bodies, but almost nowhere have they cultural dominance by weight of numbers. A "thin spread" of members provides little base for these churches that have long histories in America.

NEW DOMINIONS AND SECTS

What about the "new dominion" church bodies, those which came to power in the nineteenth century? Four of them dominate now. The vast majority of southern counties, with the exception of some on the Gulf Coast, have majorities made up of

Baptists of the booming Southern Baptist Convention or various black churches. The upper Midwest is heavily shaded in solid colors to represent Lutheran majorities. Utah, eastern Nevada, and southern Idaho, along with western Wyoming, make up the Mormon empire. The whole Northeast and the whole Southwest are Roman Catholic, as are the upper Great Lakes counties and most northern urban centers. These are represented sufficiently strongly that they have become very familiar and have an opportunity for contributing to cultural dominance. They are new enough on the scene not to have experienced the erosion the colonial denominations have known. The Baptists and the Mormons grew very fast. The Lutherans enlarged moderately rapidly—especially in their stronghold areas—while the Roman Catholics grew reasonably. The recent Catholic past is so full of complications that it is difficult to generalize about it.

Here are the actual growth rates from 1940 to 1970: While the United States population grew by 58 per cent, the Lutheran Church-Missouri Synod gained by 118 per cent, the Roman Catholics by 127 per cent, the Southern Baptist Convention by 136 per cent, and the Mormons by an astonishing 186 per cent. The one denomination that does not easily fit the pattern is the United Methodist Church. It does have statistical predominance in a long belt across the border states, but it gained by only 33 per cent. Born between the two periods about which we are speaking, it has a mixed record.

None of this suggests an all-purpose theory for church growth or decline. But it does propose that those churches which were established early, took custodianship of the culture seriously, and made many compromises in their career in American history or risked much in the recent past, are suffering. Who prospered? Those which were established later, as a result of nineteenth-century internal migration or Continental immigration, were not as consistently responsible for cultural expression on a national scale, stood somewhat apart or kept their inner integrity through the years, and risked less so far as clientele favor has been concerned in the social realm.

More successful statistically than these have been the denominations that never dominated, the "sects" (which have never been established). They have no counties colored or striped on the map to suggest numerical importance on localized bases. They tend to be aloof from or hostile to the culture and are uncompromising in their interpretation of it. They take few risks in the social sphere. Their growth figures are: Church of the Nazarene (131 per cent), Seventh-Day Adventists (139 per cent), Assemblies of God (224 per cent), and Church of God (332 per cent).

WHO GROWS WHEN?

The public has been well informed both by analysts and bragging success churches that the more theologically and socially conservative churches are growing, and that the others are generally declining. No one exactly defines what conservative means or what is being conserved, nor do all conservative churches grow at similarly impressive paces. In the best-known recent study, Dean M. Kelley set forth data and speculation as to *Why Conservative Churches Are Growing*. His book has become a kind of manual of arms for many church leaders, who believe they can use it to restyle their denominations in order to begin to grow at more satisfying paces.

Those churches which demand heaviest commitment, exact the hardest discipline, have the most missionary zeal, are most absolutist, call for strictest conformity, or lean toward fanaticism are growing most, argues Kelley. Those which allow for some relativism and diversity, engage in dialogue with others, tolerate lukewarmness, encourage individualism, and are reluctant to engage in missionary or proselytizing activities languish. Presumably this process has gone on for some time, since the Episcopalians, Congregationalists, and to a lesser extent the Presbyterians clearly experienced relative decline in the ranking of denominations throughout the nineteenth century. The trend is newsworthy now chiefly for two reasons: Few outside observers expected committed-disciplined-missionary-absolutist-conformist-fanatic groups to grow in that age which many have called secular. At the same time, the relativist-diverse-dialogical-lukewarm-individualist "old dominion" denominations and the Methodists have been losing place.

Religion in America seems to be a game played by innings. In the suburban splurge of the 1950s the well-recognized old churches profited and were in the news. In the turbulent 1960s these did most of the social-activist work: the demonstrating, issuance of proclamations, taking of controversial stands, the innovating in theology. Thus they were in the news. In the inning that began around 1968 the media started focusing on those which had been growing but had previously received less attention. Their enthusiasm and programmatic fervor permitted at least one kind of new news to be made and reported on.

In one interpretation, the "old dominion" groups have not been good at recruiting. They have had to be content to live in part off people who "trickle up" on the social scale; they simply have to wait for some of the new converts brought in by the more enthusiastic revival churches. The revivalists, meanwhile, will continue to do the converting. Their churches will retain most of the newcomers, but there will be some revolt, some disaffection, some upward mobility into the old, established denominations.

No one knows the future. It could be that one or another of the settled older churches may continue to decline in statistical significance to the point reached by Unitarians or Quakers, which are usually listed as "having an influence beyond their numbers." They could even disappear entirely—though that is not likely—through mergers independent of the general Protestant unitive movement. On the other hand, while it is inconceivable that any of them could get their clienteles to change their mentalities so much that they could grow on the premises shared by Jehovah's Witnesses or Latter-Day Saints—or even, for that matter, of Southern Baptists—some could renew themselves in their own traditions and learn from the growing churches of today. Nor is it possible to know how long the cultural conditions in which the conservative churches can continue to grow will persist. As they help provide ballast for an unsteady nation, they have everything going for them. Slight cultural shifts or societal realignments could make their lives more complicated.

NON-DENOMINATIONAL PATTERNS

Discussion of growth on denominational lines is partly misleading, since much of the new excitement has occurred on transdenominational or non-denominational bases. In many respects, as the ecumenical fervor has died down somewhat among the earlier ecumenical groups, it has proceeded apace in the once standoffish evangelical churches. They unite with each other, despite long histories of separation, and they link hands with Roman Catholics in support of Billy Graham crusades or, more formally, in a venture designed to produce growth, "Key 73."

The free-enterprise ventures of Christians with these points of view also prosper. While the large religion departments of the New York trade publishers sometimes tend to decline and while many established Roman Catholic publishers disappeared, the more conservative book houses in the Midwest reported booming sales through prospering bookstore chains. While many denominational and most expressive independent religious magazines declined or died, Billy Graham's *Decision* circulated by the millions. The historic university-related divinity schools or major denominational seminaries cut back to meet declining markets for their highly trained graduates and to live within their inflationary budgets. The intransigent evangelical independents and some denominations of their type expanded. They attracted more seminarian and clerical "tentmakers," more people who make much of their living off secular employment, are more mobile, their education and professional life less expensive.

The major denominational youth programs came into bad times. Campus Crusade, Young Life, Youth for Christ, and countless Jesus- and Pentecostal-based movements added to their staffs. Needless to say, being conservative does not offer a sure-fire formula for growth. Many ventures that can be characterized by that adjective fail or remain pathetically weak. Not all less conservative groups or ventures declined. There are impressive exceptions. But the media have discerned the general pattern, and the public is getting the picture.

The fast-growing groups tend to have non-member friends in high places. While many of them are lower on the social scale, they tend to be befriended by people of affluence and supported by people in power. They may very well thereby have begun the act of compromising or of taking responsibility for cultural directions that hurt their predecessors. In the meantime they enjoy the luxury of playing the growth game for all it is worth. Whereas in the sixties a typical national newsmagazine's religion section would feature social experiment or theological risk, in the 1970s it more frequently reported on huge new tabernacles built by successful evangelists, growing Sunday schools, or ec-static youth movements.

The growing groups are not exempt from some of the prob-lems their more sluggish counterparts have known. Will their own new ecumenical involvements not lead to some diversity if not relativism, dialogue if not lukewarmness, individualism if not reserve? Will some of them have theological second thoughts about simply providing society with its ballast, and begin to do some upsetting? Some signs are present to suggest that they have begun to do so. Will not the new dominion experienced by a group like the Southern Baptist Convention lead it to compro-mises that will result in "mere worldliness"? In many respects these signs have been on the scene already in many a southern city.

Most important, do their successes not lead them into some of the very organizational and bureaucratic problems that haunted the less aggressive churches? "Explo 72" used huge computers to program its details. The Campus Crusade organi-zation grows ever more complex and experiences more strain on the very personalism it has to offer. The Southern Baptist Con-vention founds tens of thousands of churches in a couple of decades—a venture that could not be effected simply on the basis of the Baptist's cherished old localism.

These and other issues nag the more thoughtful and self-critical leaders. In the next two chapters we shall run a kind of balance sheet on both the fast growers and the slower growers. What might the longer history teach the former and the recent past teach the latter? Working on the assumption that American religion needs both, I shall also be critical of both. It would be unfair, then, to isolate either chapter to see who is most picked on. Each has something to teach the other, if they can be chastened enough to care or lifted enough to hope.

4

Clay Feet
Clear Up to Our Navel

RESISTING THE AGE

"The spirit of the age." Again and again, American churches have thought they were resisting that spirit when in fact they were breathing it in and prospering from it. Dean William Inge of the Church of England is supposed to have said something to the effect that the Christian Church ought to calculate stead-fastly to resist the spirit of the age. In the Kennedy-Johnson years the leaders of churches that were in the news often acted as if they thought they were in the resistance. They sometimes took unpopular stands, lost friends, and were considered con-troversial. Yet the attention of the media and the public showed that they were also offering a program dictated not only by their own inner vision but by what they thought was relevant. They neglected elements of that vision if they thought it was not part of what modern secular man would consider "plausible"—to use Bishop James C. Pike's favorite word.

In the Nixon era the custodians of a different set of Chris-tianity's notes and accents have difficulty resisting the spirit of the age. A morally uncertain society seeks self-justification and welcomes either the silent assent or the encouragement of the churches. A bored and experience-starved generation in the

1970s seeks spiritual thrills and welcomes them from previously overlooked sources. A nation recovering from and reacting to upheavals solicits new stability and balance. The spirit of the age dictates, and the growing and prospering half of American churchdom responds, advertising that now this half possesses what is relevant and appropriate.

If any lessons from the revival of interest in religion in the Eisenhower era are to be remembered, the churches will have to find ways to resist temptations to go in pursuit of immediate success at the expense of an address to the whole counsel of God. So, at least, think many of the self-critical leaders of the evangelical parties and movements in the churches. In the years when the mass communicators, the prime delineators of the spirit of the age, were going easy on them, thoughtful evangelists raised questions. Bill Pannell, a member of Tom Skinner's black evangelistic crusade team, in 1970 told a group of followers, "We have clay feet clear up to our navel." And Seattle Pacific College's President David L. McKenna challenged leaders of the National Association of Evangelicals to put their ethical and spiritual commitments on the line and take some risks, "or this generation will put their commitments on the line to take us in directions we do not wish to go."

A REVIVAL WITHOUT ENEMIES

If prophetic words are to be spoken against the spirit of the age as it is being adapted to by the churches, they will come with the best credentials and most telling effect from the corners of church life that a decade earlier were being dismissed as irrelevant because they were then going against the spirit of that age. Journalist William Randolph Hearst reportedly ordered his papers to "Puff [Billy] Graham!" ("*puff* [puf], v.t., to praise in exaggerated language") when that evangelist was first coming to prominence. In the 1970s "puff evangelism and evangelicalism" might be the new media motto. The communicators will eventually get bored or have second thoughts. But, for the moment, what is colorful and exotic and responds to whatever society seeks is puffable. The Pannells and McKennas have to take up the critical role from the front.

Caesar will have no complaints. Not that America's assertive and expanding churches are unanimously gathered in support of the nation's military and nationalistic ventures or united to keep a political administration in power. There is a reasonable degree of variety in the evangelicals' ranks. But their general ethos calls for support of society's status quo or quiet assent to public policy. When the nation is for peace, they are for peace; when it is at war, they go; when it bombs, they fall silent. One can hardly blame Caesar for not being friendly to those churches which sometimes are critical of his ventures. But it should cause some worries to Christians to note that the precincts of the White House's East Room, the symbol of the political "spirit of the age," have been open only to that half of religious focus that gives quiet or vocal assent to administration policy. The king will not inconvenience such prophets; he will make chaplains of them.

What happened to the other wing of American religion? In the 1950s a theologian like Reinhold Niebuhr could still roar from Morningside Heights in New York: "Seek justice and not favor; awaken consciences and do not lull them."

Spokesmen in his lineage are now in disarray. They are dispirited or have little to say. In fact, many who survive are subdued, hungry for favor, envious of the successes of the other religious party. Where they can, they adapt to the policies of the latter and try to get going for them whatever works for their conservative brothers. Not many of the adapters will be listened

to, at least not with the same nervous attention given a few
rank-breaking evangelical scholars or politicians who go against
the time spirit.

A generation weary over division and divisiveness tends to go
easy on itself. Now and then as one watches Protestant near-
fundamentalists link up with the more intransigent Roman
Catholics, it occurs to ask: Have all the old distinctions and definitions disappeared? Thus, in a venture called Key 73, Protestant leadership welcomed the support of St. Louis' John Cardinal Carberry, the American Catholic leader most given to the
devotion of Mary as Co-Redemptrix and miracle worker of
Fatima. Will eager evangelicals pay any price, overcome any
difference, overlook any embarrassment, all for the sake of pursuit of their objectives of growth? So the Jehovah's Witnesses
and Latter-Day Saints are aggressive, growing, and successful.
Are their intentions, their methods, their theology only to be
emulated, never criticized?

Here and there, people have begun to question from within
some of the dimensions of the Pentecostal experience or the
Jesus movement on psychological and sociological grounds. To
engage in criticism of the whole trend on such bases is not our
purpose here. To examine the clay feet of the bullish denominations and forces is more in place. And the point at which to begin is the question of often the only norm that matters in the
early 1970s: the cult of growth and success.

FASCINATIONS WITH SUCCESS

When religious forces forget all else in order to grow and
when they place their highest premium on success, they have
to overlook emphases that had once been dear to them. You do
not, as a minister, stand at the side of a black couple bombed
out of its home in a white neighborhood in the middle of a

church building fund campaign. So went a truism of the 1950s. Nor do you question the bombing of civilian populations for your own nation's political purposes when you are out to win the favor of a citizenry that is weary about being criticized. Exceptions are refreshing. The minister in charge of metropolitan Chicago's Key 73 evangelism effort, the Reverend Henry W. Anderson, of La Grange's First Presbyterian Church, did just that. He and other leaders very publicly and at high risk called on Billy Graham to join them in some sort of religious gesture that would indicate a non-support of the killing. Their move had to be motivated by Christian conscience and not by calculation of a desire to curry favor. After such risks, one might only hope that Anderson-led efforts still would also win a million souls. But his kind represents an endangered species.

The fascination with success is an old one in American religion, and can be used both ways by manipulators. Curiously it often becomes tangled up with truth claims. When a religious force does not prosper, when it languishes or dwindles or falls into disfavor, its size is reckoned as a mark of its purity and the truth of its gospel. Did not Jesus say that the Church would be a little flock, that his disciples would look beleaguered and would suffer disfavor at the world's hands? "Woe to you if all men speak well of you."

When things go well and there is growth while all men speak well of a group of Christians, the temptation to reverse everything comes into play. Since American churches have grown more frequently than they have not, they have often been in position to connect their truth claims with upward lines on their membership graphs. I call this tendency McCabeism, after a nineteenth-century Methodist planner and planter of new churches, Charles McCabe. One day while on a train he read "infidel" Robert Ingersoll's boast that Christianity was on the

verge of downfall. He left the train to wire: DEAR ROBERT: "ALL
HAIL THE POWER OF JESUS' NAME." WE ARE BUILDING MORE
THAN ONE METHODIST CHURCH FOR EVERY DAY IN THE YEAR
AND PROPOSE TO MAKE IT TWO A DAY! C. C. MCCABE. The Rev-
erend Alfred J. Hough followed up with a hymn:

> The infidels, a motley band,
>   In council met, and said:
> "The Churches die all through the land,
>   The last will soon be dead."
> When suddenly a message came,
>   It filled them with dismay:
> "All hail the power of Jesus' name!
>   We're building *two* a day."

McCabe's biographer spoke for the tradition of growth and success in religions' stock markets. He thought that these exchanges rated literarily with *Pilgrim's Progress.* "Dry and subtle
arguments of academic merit, which even the schoolmen never
wasted their time to read and which the people could not understand, were very weak defences of the Gospel and very harmless answers to infidelity compared to this simple, witty, yet un-
answerably logical allegory," he said of McCabe's "Dream of
Ingersollville."

McCabeism, not the worst vice on the religious scene, possesses its own charm. Over against the groveling and self-pity of
much ecclesiastical leadership, it represents a rather winning,
cheerleading, zesty effect. Churches that are sick and tired of
hearing themselves dismissed as irrelevant every other decade
can hardly be blamed if, enjoying temporary favor, they create
bandwagon effects during the period when they represent the
center of action.

The reducing of Christianity's truth claims to the "Look, Ma, we're growing!" motif is dangerous only when it leads to loss of perspective and the creation of illusions. The fundamentalists who like to read the signs of the times buy Hal Lindsey's pop-apocalyptic pleasantry, *The Late Great Planet Earth*, by the millions and pile up awesome statistics for a religious best seller. But rather than "rejoice that the spirits are subject to them" because of this triumph, the more thoughtful minority of them glance up and down the bookstalls now and then to become aware of multimillion sales for *The Sensuous This* or *That* or *the Other Thing*. Bill Bright and Campus Crusade deserve some sort of congratulations for rallying eighty-five thousand young people in Dallas for "Explo 72." This pride can be enjoyed as they boast that this was the largest evangelistic crowd in history. But Ohio State and its competitors gather that many people without an inch of advertising space every autumn Saturday afternoon for football. The statistics game was self-defeating in the 1950s and remains so in the 1970s.

Along with the success boasts come illusions and the temptations subtly to tailor the message ever more to the spirit of the age. The danger that boredom can turn off the people who have been attracted by the bragging game is haunting. The possibility that leaders do not discern the reasons for growth or forget the original goals of Christian witness and ministry is overwhelming.

INVISIBLE GROWTH AND REVOLVING DOORS

The statistics game is especially confusing in the case of most rapidly growing groups. For twenty years and more, the nation has been told about the overwhelming potency of "Third Force Christendom." Dr. Henry Pitney van Dusen, then president of New York's Union Theological Seminary, called attention to the Pentecostal and sectarian waves that were reaching American religion's shores. It was the fastest-growing portion of Christianity—in the Caribbean, in Africa, in Latin America, in Indonesia. But claims were also made for the great growth of this force in North America. On a percentage basis the Pentecostal denominations have indeed been "young, rugged" by contrast to the "old, worn-down" ones nearby.

A citizen has a right to be impressed, after he has been cowed into believing that this is a religionless age, to see that the Assemblies of God grew by 224 per cent in three decades. This is growth comparable to that of the Methodists in the early-nineteenth century and represents an outpacing of population growth by about four times. But this really means that instead of 199,000 people in that church, there are now 645,000. Another Third Force force, the Church of God of Cleveland, Tennessee, holds a record with a 332 per cent growth rate, which is six times the population rate. The same observing citizen has reason to take notice again. Now there are 272,000 Church of God of Cleveland, Tennessee, members where there had been 63,000 in 1940. The growth rate for astrology and *Playboy* are at least as revealing cultural indicators.

What happens to all those Pentecostals about whose growth one hears each year? Since 1960, tongue-speaking has "broken out" in Catholicism, Episcopalianism, Lutheranism, and the like. The meeting of twenty thousand of these each summer at Notre Dame produces perhaps the largest continuous, automatic conference response in American religion in the 1970s. But despite the surges and the publicity, each denomination still counts its Pentecostalists in the thousands, or each parish numbers them in the couples and fews. To notice this is not to deny the validity of what these groups are about. After having criticized the success cults, one could hardly in fairness turn around and deride someone for not having grown more. The point of the observation is only to urge that Christians who are assessing their status and planning their future would do well not to get carried away by success stories out of context. They have to observe the revolving-door effect of conversion-minded groups who report on the "ins" more than the "outs," and count the "ins" as they repeatedly re-enter.

VISIBLE GROWTH AND SELF-CRITICISM

Southern Baptist growth is awesome. In the South and in some northern suburbs at least, something of the old evangelical empire lives on. This growth has not been automatic. The Convention employs an able, astute, well-motivated, and theologically alert national evangelism staff. But its evangelists are more self-critical and aware of what is going on than are the secular communicators who gasp at their growth. The planners know the denomination's advantages of dominion. Many a medium-sized southern city, for example, is a kind of theocracy. Few politicians would think of countering Baptist mores and hope to survive. Country clubs are not always present or necessary, since the Baptist and Churches of Christ groups give cradle-to-grave, morning-till-night, season-by-season outlets for approved social life. The newcomer in such a city had better greet the Welcome Wagon lady with a "Yes, I'll probably be joining one of your churches."

Since the old, worn-down Methodists also have vestiges of empire in many American regions and counties, it is appropriate to ask, "Why are they not so successful?" Or *are* they successful where empire remains, and languid only where they share a thin spread of influence in northern cities, along with Presbyterians, Episcopalians, Baptists, and the United Church of Christ? We lack data to be conclusive about this exception. Liberal theology and social activism are usually cited as reasons for slower growth.

Christians enjoy seeing their reconciling circle grow. Members of many organizations certify something of the quality of their commitments when they see their product accepted. It would be absurd to ask the growing forces to hold back and not to grow. What is appropriate is to suggest that bullishness should not lead to bravado or illusions, and that the price of growth be counted or the reasons for growth be measured by some specifically Christian norm.

Such measurement has begun to occur within these camps. At a celebrated Congress on Evangelism in 1969, evangelicals tried to do justice to more than one kind of Christian endeavor. In the Tom Skinner crusades, racial injustice is faced up to along with the idea of winning the continent for Christ. In the theology of the Donald Bloesches, Kenneth Hamiltons, Bernard Ramms, or in the social thought of a host of evangelicals who do not favor White House East Room religion or on the pages of the *Reformed Journal,* sometimes *Eternity, The Christian Herald,* and even to a lesser extent *Christianity Today,* the new prophetic voice is occasionally heard. Whispers of criticism from those sectors can be more telling and more effective than thunders from the post-Niebuhrian Protestant orbit. The presence of "People's Christian Coalitions" in evangelical colleges and seminaries and of underground papers are marks of hope when they disengage latter-day fundamentalists from support of the world as it is.

The "marks of the Church" that Dean Kelley isolated as factors helping to account for exceptional church growth are appraised by these internal critics. On one account or another, they are inclined to say, "We have clay feet clear up to our navel." They are not sure that the old marks "One, Holy, Catholic, and Apostolic" should be replaced by the new ones cited by Kelley.

THE NEW MARKS OF THE CHURCH

First among these, says Kelley, is "total identification of individual's goals with group's." That mark is effective for attracting what Eric Hoffer called True Believers. It does not allow for the Protestant principle of prophetic protest, which asks Christians to call into question first and most their own group and its goals.

"Willingness to obey the commands of [charismatic] leadership without question" is Kelley's second mark. At the *Insearch* conference in Chicago in January 1973, the charismatic leader of a successful Pentecostal commune in California was available for interviews. Even those who did not share his community's assumptions could not help but be impressed by some of its good works and elements in its ethos. But it was astounding to hear the leader say that he reported only to God. Yes, he had twelve elders. He appointed them. Could they get rid of him? "Theoretically, yes, but not by majority vote. It would have to be unanimous, and they would have to convince me that the Lord was speaking to and through them." Could newcomers, not yet part of the commune's vision and structure, raise questions? "They could to me, but not to the brothers." No pope can get away with less concern for collegiality or for the idea of consulting the faithful. Members of a half-billion-member church have a freedom that comes with distance, compromise, and internal pluralism. Young people in such a commune have no such opportunity for gaining perspective or engaging in creative foot-dragging. While this commune may represent an extreme case, it does inspire questions about what concepts of

wholeness in Christ and Christian personality are implied in
such willing assent to authoritarian control.

Kelley's third sign is "missionary zeal, eagerness to tell the
'good news' of one's experience of salvation to others, refusal to
be silenced, internal communications stylized and highly symbolic: a cryptic language; winsomeness." That linkage of
themes should not cause so many problems. People do like to
share their beliefs. So far as cryptic language is concerned,
someone writing from the academic centers of jargon should not
even raise the question about it. But articles have begun to appear that ask whether evangelicalism's missionary activities are
not often undertaken for reasons not always congruent with
New Testament motives. Still, I prefer to let that word stand
uncriticized. So much for the first three notes in "Evidences of
Social Strength."

Another Kelleyan tier of marks are "Traits of Strictness." Ab-
solutism comes first: "Belief that 'we have the Truth and all
others are in error'; a closed system of meaning and value which
explains everything; uncritical and unreflective attachment to a
single set of values." Few would disagree over the point that
such elements all help provide social cohesion and develop
strong groups. But many evangelicals have been asking whether
their colleagues—and sometimes whether they themselves—
might be confusing their grasp of truth with God's truth. The
biblical record gives plenty of warrant for asking people to hold
to the truth. It also reminds them, in St. Paul's terms, that their
knowledge is "piece-work." Now they know "in part," and such
knowledge does not give an answer to everything. The need for
Christians to sort out the accretions of habit from the authentic
heritage moves other critics from within. Does the world need
more absolutists? Are God's purposes really better served by
ever-growing numbers of competitive absolutists who reject

each other's witness—even if they thus manifest a psychological type that will attract others of the same type?

Strong groups in Kelley's observation have "conformity" as a fifth mark of the Church. He elaborates while still condensing. This means "intolerance of deviance or dissent; shunning of outcasts (*Meidung*); shared stigmata of belonging; group confessions or criticism; separatism." Some elements of all these appear in most groups, including poker clubs and genial neighborhood groups. There is no reason to single out Christians as special sinners here. Without some discipline, churches do dissolve into the surrounding world. Few conventional congregations are in danger of having too much formal discipline. But "intolerance" cannot only be expressive of a love of God's truth. It may be another personality trait that is simply dangerous when it appears in a group.

The sixth mark is "fanaticism," "all talk, no listen; keep yourselves unspotted from the world." Fanaticism is a relative term that has to be used with care. An expert on the subject, Josef Rudin, reminds us that "not every passionate exuberance . . . should be suspect of fanaticism. Let us strongly emphasize that there is a passion which not only belongs to healthy psychic behavior but which is rightly called noble since it ennobles man and gives him dignity." In the face of the bored and passionless, Friedrich Nietzsche said, "Oh, that you would become cocky; oh, if you would still have convictions." The Apocalypse (Rev. 3:15) also offers some choice words about lukewarmness. But this trait can also be pathological and have little to do with Christian wholeness.

LIABILITIES OF THE FAST GROWERS

The formulas for growth and cohesion are all present in Kelley's norms. They hardly represent much of what used to be called the whole counsel of God. They exact too high a price in Christian virtues. Perhaps the divine mission could better get along with some smaller church forces, with fewer absolutists-conformists-fanatics. So contend reflective members of the fast-growing groups. The public media are more fascinated by these absolutist-conformist-fanatic types, whether in Pentecostal communes, at campus crusades, or in congregations, than they are by those from whom Nietzsche would have exacted more cockiness and more conviction.

The *substance* of such witness matters little. "Oh, of course I don't agree with that outfit, but they at least have *some* juices flowing, something going for them. And the viewing or reading public will sit still for them, at least." Media dependence is a problem for the fast growers just as it was in the sixties for the activists.

The same reporters who picked up and puffed the Jesus freaks dropped them when they were bored or when something new came along. The tendency of the enthusiasts to certify their credentials by reference to the media and other outside forces puts them in an ambiguous spot. After hearing a group of Jesus people attack the secular world and those who are moved by it, numbers of us were startled to hear from that same group the idea that we should take them seriously because their leader had a Ph.D. Is there a more visible mark of corruption in the human family? We should listen because two newsmagazines had devoted attention to them? Self-critical evangelical loyalists have begun to argue that the terms for Christian response have to be retrieved by Christians and not set by a fascinated "outside world."

Another element in the program of the success-minded religious forces of the seventies is the single-minded accent on experience. Here again the spirit of the times and the mission of these groups are in perfect congruence. At the University of Colorado in 1971 thousands of students gathered for several days to hear every kind of guru, shaman, holy man, saint, and meditator make the case for his or her vision. Those of us in the Christian line naturally drifted into the pattern wherein we made our own case. It went something like this: Christianity also has a "dropout" lineage. This faith also inspires meditation and contemplation. Jesus retreated to the mountains, Paul went to the desert, the people in the Acts of the Apostles had communes and "gladly broke bread." St. Paul usually had to scold the congregations because they were too fervent and nearly orgiastic when they got together for a celebration. Do not be too grim, too productive, too programmatic. Do not let ethical concerns pre-empt the whole field in religion.

What each was doing, committed us to focusing concern on one element in Christianity. They left other areas neglected, other flanks exposed. Someone in the audience caught this and immediately drew some of us up short. "Do you really think that message is necessary in the 1970s? At a time when apathy and unconcern for the world and its issues are the thing to show, why do religious leaders feel it important for people to go further in the natural direction they are going anyhow? Why did you not say things like this back when the churches *did* have the opposite temptations, and needed these words? Maybe now is the time to resist the trend of the day and inspire some social action and passion."

In the midst of chatter about the experience of Jesus and the invocation of his name, it is always possible that someone can again say and be heard: "Not everyone that says, 'Lord! Lord!' shall enter into the kingdom; but he that doeth the will of my Father which is in heaven. . . ." A culture fascinated by the splattering of psyche, the tripping of tongues, the pathology of religious experience, is temporarily engrossed by people having a jag or getting their kicks—whether over drugs or sex or Jesus.

Reactors to the reactor at Boulder, Colorado, should not wish to reject hunger for religious experience. The religious vision, as already noted with less than a sense of breathless discovery, is ordinarily born of a sense of conversion, the seeing of a sudden blinding light, the experience of inner illumination and the "lighting of the fire." It is often nurtured through retreat from the workaday world and from the doings of frantic men. But that vision is expressed and tested also in a thousand gestures and effects, and particularly in the question of how one addresses the situation of the neighbor.

Self-sustaining nuclear reactions that come from the glowing center of religious life can open people to new ways of looking at the world. But conjured versions, of which there are plenty when experiences are the thing to have, can close them off. As a student of American religion, I share fascination with the new enthusiasts. One cannot really write the history of American religion without having empathy for revivalists, ecstatics, visionaries, and their followers. So the temptation comes to be a bit uncritical whenever an interesting phenomenon comes along. Such phenomena are more congenial at a distance than close up. Says a wife: "Oh, the Jesus freaks are all right; but would you want your daughter to marry one of them?" And a neighbor: "Pentecostal fervor is fun—but not next door."

Many a minister welcomes news of these outbreaks and contagions as signs of Christian renewal. He then feels his heart sink when he learns that they are spreading in his congregation. Designed though they are to unify and vivify a flock, he knows that their advocates focus on experience and frequently reject those who have come to the faith in different ways. A test for any experiencing group should be: is anything that is not utterly narcissistic, utterly self-indulgent present in what unites them?

A corollary or accompaniment of the tendency to narcissism is the frequent simplism that motivates not only the enthusiasts and ecstatics but also the more straight-and-square growing groups. Those who have lived with simplism for a long time probably have counted the cost. The naïve newcomers who can least be reached, most need to be. The young Jesus person, age seventeen, a protected suburbanite from a middle-class home, says: "I was really world-weary. I had tried *everything*. Then I came to Jesus. He answered all my questions. He is the 'one way.' He is all I need. Don't complicate my life with anything complex. Faith in him is simple, and as long as I feel good about it and him, that's it." Here is a short-circuiting. She may have experienced several things: a bit of marijuana, a little sex, a high school course on world religions, an evening with an older sister who was in the SDS back in its prime. But most blacks, ghetto residents, white ethnics, members of developing nations, custodians of Christian tradition, fellow Christians, intellectuals, and the rest of the world would hardly admire her for such short-circuiting, which cuts her off from so much possibility.

THE SIMPLE AND THE COMPLEX

The Christian life allows for and enjoins simplicity. "Simplify, simplify. . . ." Thoreau's words can be drawn into the religious orbit. But Alfred North Whitehead better informs Christian life: "Seek simplicity, and mistrust it." The psychic overload of the young American who finds Jesus or of the middle-aged suburbanite who feels the Spirit is understandable and has to be ministered to. When a person begins to find illumination and patterning in a random and chaotic world, a "saving" experience occurs. That emotion represents the end of the quest, so far as many are concerned. Some responsible evangelical leaders stepped back from "Explo 72" because it displayed so little sense of the ways in which Christians are connected with a world of physical need and injustice, or because so little thought was given to "loving the Lord with all one's mind."

Confrontation with Jesus people: "Professor, you probably are Christian, but you are too intellectual." The professor mutters back: "Intellectuals don't think so, but I know what you're trying to say." "Yes, you make everything so complicated, everything so interconnected. Jesus takes you away from all that. Completely forget everything else." Professor: "Where did you get that idea?" "The Bible, the only place to learn about the 'one way.'" Professor: "O.K. I'll accept the premise about the simplicity of the gospel. Is Paul all right in your book?" Answer: "Of course, he was one of the *real* Jesus people—didn't you ever read about his experience of the third heaven?" Professor: "Yes. Have you read about his subsequent task of interpreting?" The kids: "What do you mean?" Professor: "Let's look at Paul's Letter to the Colossians, in *your* book:

> 'Christ is the image of the invisible God, the first-born of all creation; for in him all things were created, in heaven and on earth, visible and invisible, whether thrones or dominions or principalities or authorities—all things were created through him and for him.'

All things—that takes people back also to the libraries and zoos, galleries and museums and laboratories." "Well, maybe . . ."

Well-rounded religious intellectuals are sometimes put off by what they take to be the rationalism of some evangelical apology. They might do well to be a bit more gentle in criticizing the work of the Inter-Varsity group and others who are at least trying to connect the Christian experience to an intellectual framework—even if that framework is a bit propositionally neat for some tastes. It does recognize a responsibility and opens the door for further elaboration.

Unless such enterprises occur within the circle of enthusiasts and fast growers, simplism will remain. If history provides any clues at all, the exclusive appeal to emotion can be effective for a moment. Then it creates other difficulties or fails to do justice to Christian fullness. A famous passage in Alfred North Whitehead's *Adventures of Ideas* still haunts the pietist world, inspiring those who have hearing ears and leaving the closed-off unmoved. The philosopher there referred to the Methodists of earlier England, but the approach he described applies again and again to evangelical forces. They "appealed to the direct intuitions" of workers and the new middle classes. "They appealed to the toiling, isolated groups of pioneers," and did them a service in America that, Whitehead says, is still often overlooked. "They brought hope, fear, emotional release, spiritual insight. . . ."

In the history of ideas "the great danger is oversimplification," he went on. The movement succeeded chiefly because it came at the right time—just as today's enthusiasts can exploit a climatic change. The movement "more than deserves the eulogies bestowed on it. But it can appeal to no great intellectual construction explanatory of its modes of understanding. It may have chosen the better way. Its instinct may be sound. However that may be, it was a notable event in the history of ideas when the clergy of the Western races began to waver in their appeal to constructive reason." "The movement was singularly devoid of new ideas, and singularly rich in vivid feelings."

Evangelical intellectuals who point out the necessity for

frameworks of interpretation of the vision often feel that they are spitting into the wind when they urge on their colleagues the role of bridge building to the disciplines and vocations of men. Their strictly historical argument has little effect. But the long future of their movement depends in no small part on the degree to which they can help people take a simple experience and connect it somehow to "all things" that "were created through Christ and for him." This need not mean that the movement would be better off if everyone turned intellectual. It would mean that people at the very least need not lower their intellectual curiosity or aesthetic senses when they "come to Jesus."

THE WORLDLINESS OF THE OTHERWORLDLY

If simplism is the problem of the enthusiasts, an often lightly disguised worldliness marks the career of many who become parts of the fast-growing "new dominion" churches or more settled sects. The joiners would be surprised to hear that they have anything to do with the world. The marks of the Church that Dean Kelley saw in their approach imply a belligerent turning from the world. But the larger society sees all but the most radical few as worldly in conventional terms. Their chosen rhetoric of deferred benefits and otherworldliness is misleading. British sociologist of religion David Martin did not let anyone get away with the illusion. "Nor would belief in a world hereafter prevent proper and successful attention to events here and now. A Texan Baptist millionaire for example would not necessarily fix his eye singly and solely on the appropriation of deferred benefits."

We are back to the old questions: Who in the world opposes a Billy Graham? Not businessmen, politicians, media people, athletes, agnostics, gossip columnists, entertainers, or the public which annually finds him "the second most-admired man in America." Who is against him? A few scattered, precious clerical critics, chiefly nowadays from his right. Maybe a producer of pornography would be angry if it could be shown that Graham's preaching against his vice actually hurt his business. But powers that be have no reason to oppose him, since he does not really undercut worldliness. Styled a prophet by others, he has latterly styled himself only a New Testament evangelist and not an Old Testament prophet, thus relieving himself from the burden of attacking most social injustice.

The less-worldly-than-thou game is simply the obverse of the worldlier-than-thou version current in the previous decade. No one has credentials or even proper definitions to play it. In worldlier-than-thou days, Christian intellectuals, claiming that the gospel called them to be secular, had difficulty showing how their embrace of the world as it is was different from the program of the Positive Thinkers whom they were rejecting. Now the critics of the evangelicals' worldliness lack credentials, because they also have made their own compromises and have uncritically enjoyed the material world. The best they can do is to have the otherworldly world-embracers come to admit that their own signal is ambiguous.

To achieve this, everyone has to step back first to find perspective. The question: Has not the note of prophecy against the powers and against the nation's way of life not disappeared from successful evangelicalism? Should Christianity *only* contribute to the ballast of society, or should it now and then overturn something or knock it off balance? The evangelical tradition has long been credited for its ability to point to individual vices, knowing that these can lead to spiritual attrition. But by its virtually complete adherence to the worlds of the powers-that-happen-to-be in politics, business, and the like, it remains a bewilderment to the tiny minority of its internal critics.

The this-worldliness of the movement shows up most regularly and surprisingly in the apocalyptic circles. Those who once upon a time were devoted enough to expectation of Christ's Second Coming to form sects around the area were sometimes ready to prepare themselves by inconveniencing themselves. In the seventies they enjoy reading Lindsey on Satanism and Second Comings, using their knowledge to interpret the daily papers and telling people that there is nothing to do in the face of doom. Paste a bumper sticker about the "Rapture" on the back of the Lincoln Continental and do without liquor—but eat well —and enjoy! Those who do not share the Lindseyan vision or that peddled by scores of radio preachers may be no less worldly. Some of them even need theologians inventing "theologies of play" in order to give them good consciences for purposes of frolic and dance and celebration. But an interesting moment in the history of Western apocalypticism has occurred when the anticipators in no way inconvenience themselves or embarrass their neighbors.

Worries about enthusiasm and evangelicalism should be left to those who have credentials for worrying about them, about their taste, their devotion to "plastic" culture, beauty queens, the violence of professional football, and other middle-range vices. Those who may not fully share their approach to religious life can also be faulted on any of these scores, and much criticism of this type is born more of intellectual rejection of the middle and lower-middle class than of anything that can be clearly measured by broadly accepted (e.g., biblically based) Christian norms.

ANOTHER CYCLE OF LIFE

The prospering Christian movements in the early 1970s stand out because the background is so colorless. In a time when nothing happens, among them something seems to happen. When nothing works, they seem to have something working. If the past is any precedent, this ecclesiastical domestication of the generalized revival of religion in recent years will soon consolidate its gains, breed reaction, and start a new cycle of denominational life. Before long, the interpreters within these communions and communes will recognize a need to make connections with a larger world. Some—though not necessarily the majority —of the younger generation will rebel and drift away or move into the "old, worn-down" denominations. More likely, pluralism will grow in their midst. The ecumenism of Key 73 may also be a sign of a less sectarian future for many of them. They will have to face again the subtle but eventually overwhelming secular forces that will be presented to them by distracting four-day weekends, insulating high-rise apartments, and mundane preoccupations.

In the meantime the gifts their movements bring to the Christian whole can be appreciated and in part emulated by others. The slower-growing denominations may not successfully pick up the highly sectarian, absolutist, and conformist ways on which the bullish groups depend. Perhaps they should not. Something else in the catholicity of Christianity could be overlooked if all went the way of enthusiasm, ecstasy, or hard-driving evangelism and churchiness.

Most of them should be recognized as not having been nasty. Strange as this subject may sound, it ought to be brought up. "Sure," says the friend, "you have all been trying to get Billy Graham and his kind to take a more active part in judging these administrations. You think he may be compromising and easing the consciences of the President and others. Maybe he is. Think how life would be if he had chosen to be really mean, if he really believed in carrying America as far to the right as he could." Graham is not alone. While it would be hard to separate the evangelicals from the American whole—so far as can be told, they vote in almost perfect consistency with the non-evangelicals at their side on many issues—many of them soon lost the crusading fervor that could have made Vietnam a holy war or could have helped produce a Fascist Amerika. Those who are reluctant to utter self-fulfilling prophecies or speak in the imprecise terms to which apocalypticism calls us, have not been able to predict that America will turn "Fascist." If it should turn, we do not know whether it will need the symbols of conservative American Christianity to assure us that everything is all right.

Those who see tendencies toward such a national move in the general tightening of the freedom of the press and of other liberties of expression, or in the decline of concern for expressing human equality—all in the name of security—will be cheered at the growing inner diversity in the statistically successful churches and the colorful movements. They are glad for the journal *Spectrum* among the Seventh-Day Adventists, *Dialogue* in Latter-Day Saintsdom, or *The Reformed Journal*. These journals let the public know that not everyone in their camp is politically predictable. Those who look for a new social conscience in American religion take cheer from the presence of the honest historians and social thinkers who engage in quiet witness in southern seminaries and evangelism boards. While the churches that neglected "soul" and took clienteles for granted in the 1960s may not easily be able to turn enthusiastic or successful, the evangelical complex may well learn again to work for justice and to interpret more of the faith in a changing culture. The ancestors of its leaders have done so before, and there are resources present again for such a move. If a turn comes, it will entail high risk but could be backed by reasonable power.

5

Without
Boundaries or Center

Some days the observer of American religion must gain the impression that the combination of enthusiastic movements and growing denominationalism represents "the only show in town." Mass media have noticed these and given them their hour under the cameras and on the printed page. They advertise themselves as the only true embodiments of Christianity. The juice is there. They have much going for them, drawing as they do a number of authentic strands in the Christian past but also ministering as they do in the "spirit of the age," giving society what it wants and providing ballast in a time of instability.

How long the current spirit will prevail and how long the current show will be on the road, no one knows. How large the small pond of Christian enthusiasm will turn out to have grown in the landscape of American pluralism is also difficult to project. As full as denominational magazines may be with stories of the new spiritualist movements and however regularly news-weeklies or religion pages of daily newspapers turn to them for excitements, for the most part the world goes on as it did before.

Wars are prosecuted as if there were no Christian witness for peace available. Business, commercial, and industrial leaders are in no way inconvenienced by the current forms of religious fervor. Patterns of living based on traditional morality—the nuclear family, marriage, conventional sexual mores—are being displaced at their usual pace. A foreigner could visit America and, unless he moved in the culture of Sunday morning or entered the enclaves of the revivalists, he would not recognize that a way of life was being challenged or even addressed.

Other shows have been on the road. Another set of churches and leaders, spokesmen and followers, have through the decades taken on the responsibility of relating Christian witness to the powers that be, interpreting these where possible and denouncing them where necessary. Black churches have done these things in and for their community. Historic Roman Catholicism often served well in this capacity. So did Protestant churches that once had held dominion and later remained part of an informal establishment to survive and minister to America in particular ways.

For a variety of reasons associated with the world-wide movements of racial assertiveness, the black churches have been able to keep something of their relative position in America. Because of an international trauma, Roman Catholicism has sometimes had to become so self-preoccupied that its voice is uncertain. But witness remains significant there too. The churches that have sometimes been considered to be the Protestant mainstream, it can plausibly be argued, have themselves to blame for their troubles. While the historical moment and the cultural tendency have by no means favored these forces, few of them would deny that they contributed to their own difficulties.

STRANGE REACTIONS AND ABDICATIONS

When people know, really know, that they are in part the cause of their own troubles, they are tempted to react in strange

ways. First, they may be so exhausted that they enjoy the ab-
dication of power, and relish a misreading of the signs of the
times so that they do not have to pick themselves up. Future
historians may well look back on these religious voices of the
late 1960s and early 1970s and suggest that they were silent
just when they had been needed, when their moment had
come.

Sample: At a time when millions of people described themselves as being ready to explore alternative styles of community
and different ways of relating to each other, the West's oldest
and most continuous embodiments of such styles, the Roman
Catholic religious orders (nuns, monks, and the like) lost faith
in their future and began to disintegrate. *The Critic* noticed
that the 1972 Official Catholic Directory counted a loss of 740
priests, 416 brothers, 6,731 sisters—in whose vocations the society could conceivably believe—but saw a gain of nine bishops,
a vocation with which the seekers had more difficulty.

Item: For a decade, thoughtful people had tried to counter a
culture of overproductivity and frantic running around by centering their lives, meditating, or contemplating the ways of God.
In the Western world it happened that there was a tradition of
competence in this field, a continuity embodied in Roman Catholic religious orders such as the Trappists. The public notice
given the writings of Trappist Thomas Merton, who died in
this period, provided a clue about the possibilities. But many
contemplatives lost their own vision, lost faith in themselves,
and lost the skill to represent their lore. They deserted their
monasteries. Just as the seekers for alternate styles of community
had to experiment with very ephemeral and often unproductive
styles of communes, the spiritual searchers had to go mishmash-
ing around the world, devoting themselves to fad after fashion.

Again: Norman Podhoretz of *Commentary* was not the only

person to prophesy that the world after 1968 or the world of the 1970s could "belong to the Catholics" just as that of the 1960s had belonged to blacks and other minorities. Why? Because at last America was coming to recognize the residual power in "middle America," "the silent majority," "the neglected majority," the "world of the ethnics," "consensus America," or whatever it might be called. And the agency most closely related to these vocal and restless forces had been Roman Catholicism. Many Catholic leaders agreed with Podhoretz about the form of his diagnosis. The people-who-had-been-Catholic were well poised. But he misunderstood the spirit of contemporary Catholicism, which was rapidly being dissipated and was disappearing. "Padre, where are you now, just when we need you?"

For another: There are clues that the nation would have comprehended even if it could not have welcomed a truly prophetic voice. In the 1950s the conventional churches could still produce and respond to someone like Reinhold Niebuhr, who was responsive to the words of biblical seers and sages and was at home in the mid-twentieth century. American Judaism still possessed a somewhat less well-known figure of this type in Abraham Joshua Heschel, who lived on through the movements for racial justice and through the first thirteen years of America's military involvement in Vietnam, to raise a moral voice out of the deep spiritual roots of his biblical and rabbinic tradition. Beyond these, few effective voices were to be heard.

Prophecy cannot be calculated, computerized, programmed. One cannot simply make room for a charismatic and then have him or her appear on stage. Only one or two gifted people may take on the role for a whole culture. But prophecy does appear in the context of community, and the community lost heart or competence. Would-be prophets were plentiful. But most divorced themselves so far from the contexts of community that the circles of believers took little responsibility for them and understood them poorly. Enough of the old Baptist survived in Martin Luther King to make it possible for him for some time to talk to that part of Christian America that responded to a witness that the Baptists well represented. In so far as Fathers Daniel and Philip Berrigan could convince Catholics that they spoke out of and to the Roman tradition, they had some effect. For a variety of reasons, that conviction became blurred and the Berrigans ended up looking isolated and becoming less effective. Meanwhile, the conscience of the churches was dulled, the voice of conscience muted.

Try this: America in the early 1970s, for all the malaise and melancholy that afflicted it, did give signs that its citizens were seeking values. A glance at the magazine covers and booklets racked next to cash registers at supermarkets illustrate the preoccupation. How do I bring up my children? What ought I hope for? How do I present myself? What will be the nature of community tomorrow? Here again the offerings were often faddish and sensational, the approach eclectic and cafeterial. Values were entertained and dropped with the casualness one shows in picking up and dropping other options in the supermarket lines.

Ecstatic and enthusiastic religious movements do not concentrate on the quest for values. "Coming to Jesus" takes only a minute or so and focuses all of life on the intensity of religious experience and the awareness of salvation. Pentecostal fervor sets out to transcend the value quest. The expanding churches are certainly more competent than these, but they do not always have a position or poise to contribute to the values quest. Just at the moment when the long-term custodians of the matter in the religious groups that had long taken responsibility might be of use, they deserted their own lore and themselves entered the supermarket line to engage in faddish picking and dropping. (These are broad-brush lines. There are happy exceptions, and the future probably belongs to them.)

These few examples having to do with community, contemplation, ethnicity, prophecy, and values are nothing more than samples of a principle or mechanism. I am not prepared at this time to defend every feature of the traditions in detail and am aware of the complex set of reasons for the difficulties the contemporary caretakers have with these. But the illustrations do reinforce the point that at the moment when society's needs and interests are manifest, the mainstream religious forces have lost much of their competence or interest.

MOOD, MORALE, AND INTENTION

Recovery will have to begin with a frank recognition of the problems of mood. Citizens of the seventies were often exhausted and dispirited. So it is natural that from many sectors one hears a whine—the one kind of leadership sound that makes it impossible for others to follow or be attracted. Failure of verve accompanies failure of nerve. The centrists tend to allow the Jesus people to have a monopoly on emotion. Conferences of some religious bureaucracies are rather morose gatherings under the cruel fluorescent lights of an office or in the midst of the sedations of a modern motel. Moribundity marks the attitude of participants, and a low expectation greets the agenda. The liturgies are sometimes a marked contrast—especially when an imported youth or black rock aggregation is employed to enliven these affairs that subsequently lapse back into apathy.

Measures of guilt and self-hate are often visible at the base of the mood. Sensitive white church people know that they had contributed to the very racial problems that they later tried to address at little expense to themselves. Some liberals are prepared to say that "their" side had helped produce the Vietnam War, that their best and brightest had come up through Harvard and think tanks at the Kennedyan Camelot with a strange combination of pragmatism and idealism and pride that often before had gotten America into trouble. When the war really got ugly, it is true that these religious forces parted company with its programmers, but they could not completely disassociate themselves from the patterning that had produced it.

Self-hate, another paralyzing emotion so far as usefulness in the world is concerned, often characterized these forces. Through the years after the Second Vatican Council, thoughtful observers suffered as priest after priest en route to the exit, while striking at Mother Church, showed that he was really flailing himself for his involvements in a system that no longer sustained him. His Protestant white counterparts also regularly enjoyed self-imposed whipping-boy status. Any black could come in and "give 'em hell," and they groveled. Not that there were not reasons for being and feeling guilty. Groveling simply is not the long-pull Christian response to guilt.

Ecologists came along and exaggerated one or two aspects of Jewish-Christian involvement in environmental problems. ("Have dominion over the earth, . . ." the Book of Genesis had commanded.) They could usually find a willing audience of religionists who would take on themselves the whole burden of pollution. After the Six-Day War, the Christian people of peace, some of whom had been reluctant to look hawkish on one war and dovish on another—but by no means enemies of Israel—sheepishly took on all the guilt that apologists for military involvement in Israel could heap on them. "Father, I have sinned, and have failed to sign the advertisement in the New York *Times*." Such responses fail to address the valid issues in race, ecology, and international relations. They add to the enjoyment of masochists but do not help blacks, would-be breathers, or citizens of Israel.

Only a naïve advocacy of Positive Thinking would suggest that a change of mood will solve problems. A morale change only makes a new start possible. The morose and the self-haters are aware of difficulties, but they are preoccupied with their own mood. The second step in recovery comes not with evasion of the difficulties but with a frank assessment of what went wrong. So far as outside foes and forces are concerned, a saying I once heard provides an encompassing philosophy of history: "The s.o.b.s are gaining on us." There is enough qualified pessimism in that sentence to help realists hope. "We have not yet been overtaken." But looking only at the external s.o.b. is less important than the act of trying to learn what went wrong in one's own camp, or to assess the true state of things in that camp.

CATHOLICISM'S DIMINISHED WORLD

A strangely diminished world: that is the word that summarizes the situation of Western ecumenism, Roman Catholicism, the old-dominion church bodies of America, and most of the typical-average-middling religious groups. What happened to them in the 1960s? They had become boundaryless and borderless; they lacked definition. In the eyes of some people, church groups did not adapt sufficiently to change. For, just as many others, they had overadapted. It became too difficult for members to draw on the resources of the churches, too easy for them to drift and slip away. The surrounding world overwhelmed leaders with change. Only constrictive or closed and resistant groups held their strength. No all-purpose explanation for the turn will suffice. It may take a century for people to untangle all the causes for the epochal shift. Poking around and jabbing here and there for evidences of causes and signs of recovery are first steps.

Roman Catholicism saw the most change. Some there are who see the new scene only in terms of decline and fall, of irretrievable loss. To them, there had been good old days when the Church was still intact, when it held power and offered meaning and belonging and hope. Tamperers, these explained, were responsible for disintegration. That reading is careless in its memories. Whoever takes pains to revisit the relics of the old Catholicism knows that reform had been necessary. The old version could not have held together or lasted much longer.

Who had really needed all those rules and regulations? A talk with a former nun from a strict group should convince doubters that there had been incredibly demeaning rites of obedience and ill-focused disciplines. The price people paid for holding the old church together was too high in superstition, routine, mechanization. It limited the development of personalities and required the surroundings of an innocent culture. For leadership classes, that church had depended upon young men who found the priesthood a way up and out of the constrictions of the Catholic ghetto, or up and into new status within it. Young women found religious life a similar option. But the pluralist world after G.I. bills, mass higher education, and the affluent society beckoned in too many other directions.

Vatican II represented the pulling of a plug or the breaking of a dam. The Council itself was a remarkable transition. Had its moment been able to last, the church could have found easier times. Behind the dam was the power of the superstitious, unreformed, mystical, often blindly followed church. The conciliar progressives manned the sluice gates and allowed for a fresh flow. The intransigents saw what was happening and tried to close the gates and stop the flow. God had provided a reservoir of power and meaning for the church. It had to be carefully hoarded. Some would be allowed to flow over, but most of it was to be preserved. Now Pope John and his cohorts were opening everything. The conservatives were correct, of course, in their assessment of power as the world counts power. The Italian curialists knew politics and popular psychology. Their opponents knew something about ideals of personality, regard for the brother and maybe for the gospel.

Some who attended the Council as non-Catholics can be forgiven from time to time if they let pass across the eye of the mind for a split second the thought that these were halcyon days. The Roman autumns opened a new world. A forbidding tradition was suddenly open for examination. Walls were being broken, and a person could be called "brother" where he had been stranger. The change could not be undertaken without political drama, and the villainy of the bad guys *versus* the virtues of the good ones brought its own excitement. The interpreters of Christian thought had their days. For a moment, theologians were what they most wanted to be: relevant. The world press knew that at Rome was excitement unmatched in twentieth-century Christianity, and conferred status on the proceedings.

Daily some feature or other of Christian catholicity was panoplied. Byzantine or Congolese masses at St. Peter's let one secret out. Not everywhere were Catholics confined to those drab Latin masses. Not everywhere were polity and practice uniform. The European advisers displayed a variety of ways of thinking about the faith. Not everywhere were people cooped up in the dreary catechismal world. Power remained, but it was to be channeled in new ways.

AFTER THE COUNCIL

Visitors and bishops went home. Pope Paul tried to pick up the pieces. Catholic radicals tried to push all the new openings wider. The bishops were bewildered. It was hard to administer a reformed church—as their Protestant counterparts could have told them. Theologians no longer behaved. Instead of dusting off the antiques of Catholic doctrine and seeing to it that they were all locked in place, the thinkers began to become innovators.

Some mistakes were major. The Council provided an excellent rationale for the laity. They were the People of God, no longer inferiors who existed to supplement clerics and hierarchs in the rounded-off definition of the church. They could go where the clergy could not, to represent Christ in the world. And there was a new charter for the bishops, who had tried to take care of their power with concepts of "collegiality." They had made it for themselves halfway. But in between these were what might be called the service forces of the church. They were caught, deprived. What organization can do well with a demoralized service force?

Those who participated in advising self-studies of Roman Catholic religious orders heard the same set of questions with wearying frequency from the restless novices. "If, as Vatican II suggests, I can serve the Lord as well by being in the world, and if I want to teach in ghetto schools, will I not be more free to do so as a lay person than as a priest or nun? What are the sanctions that go with clerical or religious status?" The church, to be sure, repeatedly mouthed the old words about the sacrament of ordination, or the importance of vows and the special status they conferred. But functionally these mattered little. It was easier to work the works of God by simply moving off into the world, where—as the jargonists of the sixties would have it—"the action was."

People moved. And in their loneliness at the boundaries, they reached for affection or sharing. To do so, they had to be released from vows and break them. The barely thinkable happened. Priests married, nuns married, priests married nuns. Let us marry and we will stay, some said. Rome did not listen. Customs were too deep and long-lasting. Would the faithful laity tolerate major change?

Controversy awaited Pope Paul. He had to make some decision on the pressing problem of birth control. Going against the majority views of his commission on the subject, he issued *Humanae Vitae,* in the summer of 1968. American theologians reacted against the Pope, while the bishops had to support him. The faithful were confused. It became less fun to be a Catholic.

One explanation for change relates to a subtle but far-reaching shift. Professor Joseph M. Kitagawa of the University of Chicago, who brings an Easterner's eye to life in Western churches, provided me with a clue one day. Roughly: "Catholicism was, among other things, a very intricate and complex web of often very trivial practices and behavioral patterns. These change through the years, and can be slightly revised or slowly tampered with. But modernizing Catholicism after the Council removed too many of them at once. It was not mindful of the ways in which the sum of these made up the grasp of the Catholic world." Tell a woman for sixty-eight years that it is a sin to eat meat on Friday and a merit to say the Rosary. Provide support for both practices in the Latin form of an apparently changeless Mass. Then suddenly forget about Friday fasts, de-

ride or play down the Rosary, and change the liturgy into ver-
nacular and even slang, and a world slips away. Theologians
and social thinkers may make little of such behavioral nuances;
these are the whole show for many of the faithful.

Matters would have been confusing enough had these internal adjustments been permitted to develop in isolation. But all
these changes occurred in the middle of the already turbulent
sixties. Something as widespread and interlocked with the culture as Catholicism is could not be immune to the revolutions
around the church. Latin America promised or threatened revolution. North Americans lined up on one side or another of such
an issue. Catholicism was troubled over racial issues at least as
much as other American agencies and movements were. The
war in Vietnam inspired a Francis Cardinal Spellman to flirt
with holy-war concepts and to bless "Christ's soldiers." Meanwhile it horrified the Catholic left into organizing the most visible and durable opposition to the killing that had been seen as
the war dragged on.

Catholicism divided over the issue. Many of "the ethnics"
were dismissed as hardhats and backlashers by the mobile left.
These radicals, when clerics, were themselves condemned as
traitors to the cloth, unworthy priests. Still another kind of po-
larizing activity was present. More and more, it dawned on the
faithful: Catholicism can change and did change. The old mystique of authority was disappearing. Good men and bad were
both divided into warring camps. People on each side had closer
alliances with non-Catholics on almost all vital matters than
they had with each other. Why bother to be together? Where is
the boundary or center? When Catholic theologians decided to
be innovators, the members were more confused than ever. The
thinkers' intent was creative enough. They wished to cast belief
in God and the love of Christ into forms that would make sense

to moderns. Burdened by too heavy an agenda and intoxicated by the front-page attention being shown them, a few celebrities made the rounds of a lecture circuit. The first year, the halls were packed and the crowds were attentive. Not many years later, the crowds had disappeared, the formerly expectant listeners came to adopt an attitude that suggested that the theological emperors had no clothes. The thoughtful professionals became more professional and more specialized. They talked chiefly to each other. Theology lost status. No longer was it either the caretaker of old dogma nor the effective means of interpreting the new world, so far as most people were concerned.

Catholic book publishing and journalism became part of that strangely diminished world. In the mid-sixties the ecumenical opportunity had attracted attention to the publishers' products. The jet-set theologians' works sold well for a season or two. But the market shifted. The old marketing staple, the "black book" department, dwindled, as fewer people sought the old reliable missals and breviaries. The main purchasers, priests and nuns, were leaving rectory and convent. If they stayed, their budgets went into *Saturday Review* or secular novels. Boundarylessness was again the occasion for change. For a brief moment the press that had covered change prospered. *The National Catholic Reporter* came to prominence as an interpreter of upheaval. But after reporting on the first marriage of a priest to a nun, the first marriage of a bishop, what could editors do for an encore? The conservatives did not want to read such news, and the rest of the church found it of increasingly less importance.

Some Catholics bided their time by reaching out for what was new each year. A history of late-1960s fads could show that usually about a year late the Catholic avant-garde would take up fading causes with zeal. All the "big M's" had their following after the Vatican Council: McLuhan, Marcuse, Mao, the Maharishi. Op and pop art, or masses in folk, jazz, and rock rhythms quickly replaced each other. For a split second, one heard talk about the promise of the underground church. The underground usually met in urban high-rise apartments among elites or in ghettos, as signs of protest. Some worshiping cells tried to survive priestless. Before long, the underground church turned out to represent a dignified passage out of the church toward what Bishop James Pike called its "Alumni Association," more than an alternative to the routine aboveground institution.

Inflation, recession, changes in taxing patterns, decline in the number of teaching sisters, difficulties on church-state matters, changes in attitude on the part of suburban Catholics, were a few of the reasons for the decline of the Catholic parochial school. The school had been the center of American Catholic culture. Its seasons were more vivid to most of the faithful than were any other features of parish life. The winter festival, spring raffle, summer fair, and autumn bazaar designed to support it rivaled the regular church year in Catholic sentiment. Loyalties were developed in the school system. Marriages were arranged for among acquaintanceships formed there. Ghetto walls remained because of the schools—even in the apparently wall-less ghettos of the 1950s. And now they, too, were falling.

While not quite as significant in the over-all Catholic complex, the Catholic college was also in trouble. So were non-Catholic institutions of higher learning, particularly the private and religious ones, by the end of the 1960s. But once again the decline in the low-paid work force supplied by religious orders coupled with the sense of freedom that *not* going to a Catholic campus provided many, led to special problems in the church.

Add to this the problem of the youth rebellion in the late 1960s. During Vatican II nothing was more enjoyable than presenting the Christian faith in lectures or classes on a Catholic university campus, a Fordham or a Notre Dame. Two or three years later a speaker could have found few less desirable arenas. In 1968 it would have been more pleasurable and rewarding to speak up for Christ at Hebrew University or Brandeis or to interpret the church at Berkeley and Columbia than at most larger Catholic campuses. The young were working off Oedipal rage or working out their identity crises vis-à-vis Mother Church. A raging former priest, James Kavanaugh, received a standing ovation at Notre Dame while serious Roman apologists were shunned or hooted. Those days are now past. No longer is it fun to kick a wounded church. A generation has already come to college without bearing the stigmata and mixed benefits of ghetto identity formation.

The visitor to small Catholic colleges could almost hear the "whoosh!" of escaping power and potential. I spoke at Maryknoll College near Chicago thrice in four years during and after the Council. The second crowd was half the size of the first, and the third half the size of the second. Since the whole student body was at these lectures, the declining crowd was not necessarily a comment on the lecturer's failing abilities. It represented the dwindling size of a school that never made use of a spectacular new wing built during the days of Vatican II, when people were expecting new vocations to the priesthood. A visitor could rattle around in echo chambers at beautiful new seminaries near Boston—now Gordon-Conwell, a mildly fundamentalist, waxing Protestant seminary—or near Madison, Wisconsin. He or she could enjoy the fervor and competence of the sisters at Marillac College in St. Louis, and know that the school was disappearing in spite of its excellence. The great Jesuit theological school that moved from Woodstock, in suburban Baltimore, to Morningside Heights, in New York, carried with it the signs of death; the death was not long in coming. Community could not be sustained or supported on the voguish but well-intended terms that Woodstock was embodying in Manhattan.

BALANCE SHEET ON CATHOLICISM

No more villains populate this Catholic story than they do most other dramas of change. Too many alternatives were necessary and salutary for anyone to dismiss the efforts as being all misguided. They have not been without good product. Pope John could probably not have administered the reformed church much better than has Pope Paul, though John's generous spirit may have attracted some loyalties that Paul could not. The Pope may be shortsighted and many bishops ill-equipped pastorally. Many theologians were faddists, and the laity expected too much too soon.

But villainy? There may have been a little in the hearts of those who were thoughtless about the sufferings of people unprepared for change. How was it to be a fifty-five-year-old priest, a sixty-five-year-old nun, or a seventy-five-year-old grandfather looking out at threatening experiments on all hands? Maybe there was villainy in some of the set-jawed and tight-lipped conservatives who would find ways to resist all forms of innovation—and thus only add to churchly disintegration. Villainy is certainly too strong a word to use to describe a third problem, over which mere mortals could have had more control, a naïve and innocent secular romanticism. Many believed that life in the secular city would be enriching while it was impoverishing in the church. They dreamed that somewhere out there freedom came cheaply, while in the church it was dear, and hoped that available community existed everywhere but in the church.

Surprises were in store for those who made the worldly move. Many of the in-transit priests and nuns moved to the secular college or university campus because it symbolized the freedoms they sought. They there frequently became tangled in tenure disputes that made Catholic hierarchical status climbing appear to offer the freedom of the high trapeze. "The Pope could more easily reform the 600-million member Catholic Church than I could reform my six-man anthropology department," said a Catholic university president with whom I chanced to discuss the problems. A sense of self-preservation and self-importance characterized the academy as much as it had the church.

Meanwhile, just about the time the mobile Catholic leadership was finding a home in the university as the repository of values, the academy lost faith in itself. Those previously beckoning community organizations, boards, bureaucracies, service agencies, and other vocational outlets also did not turn out to be Utopia or the promised kingdom. During the campus revolts, some Catholics expressed desires to leave the university and secular employment to go back to that church which represented at least some minor power, some locale for reform, some promising malleability. Romanticism about the church would, of course, be just as foolish as it is about other institutions. People are no damn good anywhere. Such an affirmation comes closer to a base for Christian life and proclamation than does the belief that somehow, somewhere there is an island of simple meaning exempt from human foibles.

Secular romanticism was part of the general problem of boundarylessness. The center did not hold. Catholic thinkers and actors wanted to be relevant to the forces around them, but took little regard for what was their particular resource. They could be symbolized by a receiver whose antennae could take in signals and whose dials could be constantly readjusted. Few found reasons to tune in any longer. Here was a magnetic needle afloat on a viscous base, excellent at locating the pole of action. But it lacked the axis.

Much endures in Catholicism, and much can be reconstructed. Not everyone who stayed represents the intransigents. Not only the arrogant traditionalists who banner *Triumph* magazine or the frightened loyalist pillars who publish and read *Twin Circle* survive, though they, too, have a place in a church catholic. Too much vitality remains among those who weathered the storm for one to dismiss the potential for tomorrow's Catholicism.

Catholicism as the changeless rock is gone. The reference point that all other Christians could use as a measuring base for their own paces and distances has slipped or been shattered. Catholicism as a bloc is going. The ethnic voting forces are united by too many realities other than those of the church and distracted by too many attractions outside the church to be listed as an expression of Catholicism pure and simple. But neither rock nor bloc will be missed if tomorrow's Catholics try to recover a sense of centering or coherence.

Peter Schrag once put it well: The liberal Catholic who was discontented had someplace else to go. The university, American Civil Liberties Union, racial-justice organizations, new politics, and the like beckoned. The ghetto Catholic was more confined. He would be ministered to or he would sulk and drop away into the faceless crowd. When the liberal Catholic again finds the church to be one of his or her "places to go" because it offers meaning, belonging, and power, the pluriform Catholic church can survive and offer hope.

THE LESS DRAMATIC PROTESTANT CASE

That suddenly diminished world also reaches much of Protestantism, though with slightly less dramatic force. For those impressed by denominational statistics—by no means the most important though perhaps the most easily isolable and measurable factor—it is clear that the trends were set long, long ago for all the churches but Methodism.

The "old dominion" colonial big three of Congregationalism, Presbyterianism, and Episcopalianism had yielded relative positions to the frontier churches early in the nineteenth century. By 1820 the Methodists pulled away into first place, not to yield until the 1920s, when their rival, the Baptists, who had both more southern and more black strength, overtook them in Protestant ranks. The Disciples of Christ cluster passed up the Congregationalists around 1850 and the Episcopalians in the 1950s. The Presbyterians and all others except the Methodists and Baptists were passed up by Lutherans (and, of course, by Catholics) around the beginning of this century. To speak of a new relative decline among the old-line powers, then, is inaccurate. The relative decline is of long standing.

Dean Kelley, who keeps tab on such matters, has charted the ways in which the trends have continued in recent years, when a few other denominations have joined the old-dominion decliners. His graphs show arcs whose lines rise and drop like Roman candles on a summer's night as they make their way from around 1958 to 1970. The graph lines of the United Methodist Church, the Episcopal Church, the United Presbyterian Church, the Lutheran Church in America, the United Church of Christ, the American Lutheran Church take that shape.

Meanwhile the more rigid but assertive Southern Baptist Convention's, and the smaller and tighter Seventh-Day Adventists', Church of the Nazarene's, and Jehovah's Witnesses' graph lines move ever onward and upward. The moderate Christian Reformed and Lutheran Church-Missouri Synod lines show general growth and then a tapering toward decline late in the decade. This trend is also the case with the Presbyterian Church in the U.S. One can almost picture the conclaves of Reformed, Missourians, and southern Presbyterians lusting after the Jehovah's Witnesses' zooming graph lines and telling themselves to tighten up so that they can grow like those really standoffish people do.

Social analysts and theologians will be spending time for years dissecting these matters case by case. Many non-theological factors, including economics, came into play. The liberal urban, university-related seminaries are frightfully expensive—the study of divinity rates second only to medicine in costs for graduate education, in part because of its dispersal in so many relatively small schools. But the rural seminaries that form conglomerates and clusters to move to the city find that they cannot engage in much cost cutting either. Churches that have tried to make elegant architectural statements are less adaptable than the Assemblies of God or Nazarenes, who usually build simple and functional, if often ugly, meeting halls.

Economics is not the whole show, of course. The nature and character of the witness plays a part. I can almost hear the Jesus person, new style, breathing over my shoulder: "Don't beat around the bush. The churches that *really* believe in Jesus and really speak God's word with authority and really experience the Holy Spirit grow, while those that are humanist or mealymouthed have nothing to offer." If my response were, "And those successful churches also often are betrayers, because they reinforce a very corrupt society and provide justification for some very evil prejudices," it would not be wholly satisfying to him, as his whisper or taunt is not to me.

He has to be asked, What is it really to believe and preach and experience? Who gives him the authority to determine what is "real" here? Are his "fundamentals" all that fundamental in the Scripture, assuming as we both might that the Scripture is the source and norm for our debate? Are his churchmen doing justice to the whole counsel of God and the partiality of man's grasp? If he listens, we converse and both grow. If he does not, he remains absolutist-conformist-fanatic, and his church or movement grows.

Other complications enter any analysis. Do the Christian Reformed, Missouri Lutherans, and southern Presbyterians care slightly less about Jesus and God and the Spirit than do the Jehovah's Witnesses or the Church of God of Cleveland, Tennessee, both of which could teach everyone else a thing or two about growing? Would my friends' forebears or descendants in small sects agree to the standards of ordeal-by-size and test-of-truth-by-growth? Might they not see that exploitation of a moment in culture is a reason for the growth of some units, while the willingness to take on some really difficult divine mandates and some really unpopular causes may play a part in declines of others? Have not the "peace churches"—Mennonite, Church of the Brethren, and the like—been as faithful in witness and zealous in their works as the Southern Baptists for a much longer time than the Southern Baptists, without experiencing comparable growth?

The debating positions are unconvincing on both sides. Neither is likely to examine his own failures if one uses success to boast and the other defends his failure by pointing to the passing moods of the surrounding culture. More fruitful is an examination of some of the factors over which one can have control. The problem of boundarylessness of the mainstream religious forces is a fruitful beginning point. Their sprawl or the dribble of their energies into the surrounding world is a basic issue. To raise it is to imply that some task of centering—which does not mean finding the middle of the road—is before them.

A DIVISION OF LABOR

The churches in question could justify themselves as part of a cycle of life for many American Christians. Thus they would find that imposition of too-clear boundaries should limit part of their mission. The creative religious leaders of the 1950s were more often than not products of fundamentalism or conservatism in general. Many of them had come from the South or the Midwest, the two Bible belts of American mythology. Some had once been converted at back-country revivals. They later developed skills to go with their fervor, and they hit the circuit. But they also eventually thought about what they were doing. They saw difficulties with the limited shape of their mission, which was confined to extricating people from the world and packaging them for heaven.

These people-in-transit began to ask whether something in their faith did not impel them also to take on the drastic problems of the world. Did it not invite them to express themselves in arts and literature? Were they not to interpret an opening world? Some of them simply reacted and left the churches, disillusioned and embarrassed and enraged. But more of them found in theological neo-orthodoxy or a similar formula a way to hold together their profound faith and their openness to a world. They made their way into the major seminaries or divinity schools. Before long, they were expressers of Protestant witness in the larger culture.

A few of these spokesmen may have been second-generation members in WASP clerical lineages, but third- and fourth-generation leadership had become rare. For the most part, the main-line churches did not reproduce their own leadership. They needed the infusion brought by the denominations that stressed conversion. Few of these excelled at theological interpretation, cultural expression, or social action. A reporter friend accuses me: "You say you don't believe in laws of history, but you seem to think here of a kind of law. One set of churches does the converting and the other the expressing. One group does the recruiting and another makes use of the recruits. One initiates while the other waits; then the other has to initiate all over again."

No law of history operates here, but observation turns up this feature with surprising frequency. The process may not remain forever, though in some form or other it will last long. Nor should the observation let the moderate denominations and the old-line churches "off the hook" so far as witness and outreach are concerned, any more than the rigid churches should be allowed to content themselves with counting gains and not taking risks while catering to the world in the language of otherworldliness. But in any catholic, or interactive, model of the church, a model that makes much less of denominationalism than do the current growth-obsessed statisticians, this generational division of labor makes at least some sense.

A SIMILARLY DIMINISHED WORLD

All the talk about denominational growth or decline does nothing to detract from the vision of the diminished world for organizational ecumenical Protestantism. In the late 1950s, the leaders of this school of Protestantism would be regularly invited to be represented at conclaves such as those held by the

Center for the Study of Democratic Institutions. These were "summit meetings" with Jews, Catholics, and secularists. Scarred veterans look back now on these conclaves and recognize that actual power was still then being bartered. Voting blocs and residual loyalties stood behind the mystiques whose lore was being rehearsed. Matters of church-state relations were at stake. In subtle, trickle-down ways, religious attitudes toward democratic life were being altered as a result of such historic confrontations.

In those years even as few as forty people could get together at, say, a "Four C's" conference of Columbia School of Journalism, *Commonweal, The Christian Century,* and *Commentary.* They could be self-appointed and anything but representative voices for secular, Catholic, Protestant, and Jewish points of view. But in the exchanges at such conferences one could sense at least a modest transmission of power. Msgr. Francis J. Lally, editor of the Boston *Pilot,* the archdiocesan newspaper, might come to a new and different understanding of what Protestants had at stake in legislation about birth control in Massachusetts. He would leave the conference to propagate fresh views about Catholic voting—with possible effect on the electorate. Today those blocs or loyalties and the credibility of the spokesmen have all been called into question.

The National Conference of Christians and Jews convoked interfaith conferences in the early 1960s. What was said and done there had an effect on pluralism and prejudice in ways that are inconceivable now. The National Council of Churches' conferences and programs produced a different kind of consequence than they would now. Rightly or wrongly, they assumed a clientele support that has since partly disappeared. They attracted talent that had to be reckoned with. Most important, they quickened certain anxieties or fears and inspired a certain backlash among those who opposed their basic purposes. Today opposition comes only from the few who find it worthwhile to exaggerate the menace of anything that is not right wing and to exploit it for their purpose. For the rest, who is afraid of the Center, the Four C's, the Conference, or the Council today?

In the early 1960s, religious publishers in, say, Grand Rapids may have been respected in a quiet way for their custodianship of conservative Reformed theology out there in the low-rent districts, but the world that mattered was in New York. The Protestant Church-Owned Publishers Association and the Associated Church Press represented highly successful publishing ventures. Some P.C.P.A. firms and some New York publishers still do well, employing extremely inventive techniques. They experiment with various media, bend sometimes toward the evangelical-fundamentalist market, put out song books for Jesus people, and somehow hack together an audience. But few of them can rely on a stable of salable theologians or serious religious thinkers to attract a readership. No one has come along to replace the thinkers who attracted a readership only a decade earlier: Barth, Berdyaev, Buber, Bonhoeffer, Bultmann, Brunner, Baillie, whose works competed with editions of Augustine, Anselm, Aquinas—to mention only the A's and B's.

What sell now are books about Satan and the Second Coming, about revivals and "soul." But no wise publisher is likely to sit back in security, because he knows the suddenness of changes in taste and has to be alert. He can take no loyalties for granted. The religious periodicals found that they prospered best among people for whom a denomination or movement in religion represented an intact real or whole world. The better they became at addressing larger problems and mediating to the larger culture, the more their subscription lists declined. Diocesan newspapers and official organs retreated, becoming ever more safe and stereotyped. They declined while revivalist promotions took up the slack and sold by the hundreds of thousands. In an age when railroad passenger trains virtually disappeared and when *Life* magazine died, it was not surprising that other, less well-financed institutions had to contemplate demise and even to suffer it. Nothing lasts.

If there has been decline in the easily observable leadership ranks, this often reflects changes of attitude in the support groups. Just as the members of the open-ended churches had other places to go, they also had other places to give. Wealthy Christians in what some critics dismissed as the limousine-liberal set might survey the scene and decide that a black scholarship agency needed funds more than did an Episcopal seminary. Foundations, once more readily attracted to some experimental religious causes, were often themselves victims of new legal impositions. They were under greater pressure to show immediate social effects of their grants. Does one support a ghetto school or a liberal religious publishing venture or educational agency?

Only as these potential donors took a second look and began to recognize the depths of the values crisis did they take second looks at the validity of less dramatic, "long-pull" outlets for their support. For a time, they had virtually deserted the scene. Meanwhile many lay clienteles of churches were put off by the courageous social stands taken by these religious agencies, or offended by their toleration for experiment and apparently wild expression. The proclamation of "the death of God" by one professor at Emory University, some said, cost the once-Methodist school millions of dollars in potential gifts. Maybe. The controversial stands taken by agencies of the National Council of Churches certainly led to measurable reaction and declining support.

When the financial squeeze came, it was only natural for the complex institutions to begin to protect themselves. They became more cautious. They dropped some of their more controversial personnel. Even when they remained courageous, they had to adjust priorities and lopped off or cut adrift more of the experimental bureaus and task forces, leaving only the safer organizational forms to survive. As a result, there were fewer outlets for the seminary graduates who had sought specialized ministries. Meanwhile the merger and clustering of congregations and economic setbacks for churches added to a general surprising and sudden situation of ministerial oversupply. The seminaries had to cut their size accordingly.

THE SURVIVORS

Good riddance, say the fundamentalists and political intransigents. America and religion are better off without those who do not consistently contribute to stability and the status quo. We need ballast, not new winds, goes that argument. Yet it can also be shown, as I shall do in a subsequent chapter, that American religion and life will be poorer if there is further decline of the besieged forces. The base for recovery is also present. Given the upheavals of the sixties, the vulnerability of these exposed church forces, the latitude they tolerate and the experiment they initiate, one could just as well be impressed at the number of lay people who did remain and who continued to support the causes.

The sense people have that such churches demand and deserve confrontation from left and right is a compliment to their character. When James Forman presented a Black Manifesto that sought reparations from the churches, he did not head off for First Baptist Church in Dallas. Perhaps he avoided it because he valued his personal safety. No doubt he missed an opportunity for witness and the chance to confront real power.

Certainly he was naïve about the way northern urban churches are constituted and how they relate to clienteles. But he did pay New York's Riverside Church and other open-ended churches the compliment of confronting them, even though they were supposed to be languishing.

When the West Coast Jesus people got themselves together and decided to confront the churches, they did not head off to the doctrinally rigid fundamentalist churches. Maybe they were satisfied with the degree and quality of Jesusism being proclaimed in such churches, but this is doubtful, given what we know about both groups. No doubt they could have found more potential recruits in such churches. But when they wanted a confrontation, they would head for the moderate First Congregational Church of Berkeley and similar tolerant mainstream bastions—whence the power was supposed to have departed long since.

They know the special role of these "forum" churches, the ways they are occupational gatekeepers to the secular society. People of the right and the left both get a hearing there and are received with some hospitality. Their very boundarylessness, a liability so far as growth and support are concerned, is an asset in a culture that needs churches of communication. The intact and introverted churches do not allow for such encounters.

OPEN AND CENTERED

Open-endedness brings problems other than those that have to do with meaning and belonging. They can lead some churches into a pathetic quest for relevance in the face of everything that comes along. Some of the suffering churches have appraised the enthusiastic and ecstatic movements as possible bases for their own new life. Some have tried to imitate the communes and the sects. The *Insearch* conference in Chicago in January 1973 may

have performed a creative service in this respect. Experts ana-
lyzed several score of the Pentecostal communes and Jesus opera-
tions to see what was in it for them. The over-all impression was
clear. Little was there, except the possibility of a few kicks. They
occupy the role ghettos did for liberals some years ago. In a way,
Insearch researchers were saying, "Let's go slumming and attend
a Pentecostal meeting. Those tongue-speakers are interesting."
Turned off soon by these, the mainstream "straights" were more
attracted to the representatives of "the soft revolution," the encounter groups and sensitivity centers.

Unless the direction can be reversed, and unless these open-
ended groups and forces can combine a "centering" activity
with their openness to change and willingness to respond, their
decline will continue to the point where they cannot fulfill much
of their mission in the church catholic or in Western society.
Their half of Christian work would no doubt eventually be
taken up by some creative forces that have begun to emanate
from the growing and increasingly pluralist denominations such
as the Southern Baptists and from the second generation of the
enthusiastic and ecstatic movements in Christianity. But the
price of waiting is high at a time when advocates of a more
humane world are needed at least as much as statistics-minded
church extension agents are. This story has been told thus far
without much effort at scapegoating. Pope Paul or the heads of
the National Council of Churches are not necessarily villains,
even if they have not been heroes. They have been victims of
one kind of change and have not been able to seize new initiative in history. Thus they join most of the Western world's states-
men, politicians, educators, businessmen, healers, and the like.
"Nothing works." The West Point chaplain who said that he
had put one foot in a boat called the church and one in a boat

called the military, only to find them both sinking, spoke the truth for many.

In this telling, these religious forces have appeared to be analogous to the self in Robert Jay Lifton's portrayal of boundaryless individuals. They experience the world-wide sense of "historical or psychohistorical dislocation," a "break in the sense of connection men have long felt with vital and nourishing symbols of their cultural traditions—symbols revolving around family, idea systems, religions, and the life cycle in general." In our contemporary world they often came to perceive these "traditional symbols as irrelevant, burdensome, or even inactivating," and yet they could not avoid relating to them, or having their life's process affected by them.

On these terms, avant-garde religionists of the recent past found their own resources to be irrelevant and alien or enslaving.

Lifton points to one other large historical tendency, *"the flooding of imagery* produced by the extraordinary flow of postmodern cultural influences over mass communication networks." These "permit each individual everywhere to be touched by everything, but at the same time often cause him to be overwhelmed by superficial messages and undigested cultural elements, by headlines and by endless partial alternatives in every sphere of life."

On those terms, the members of open-ended groups are receptive to many passing signals that offer them options to which they believe they can become relevant and that they hope will be congenial or enslaving.

In neither case did these groups take the course of catering to or becoming representative of Lifton's alternative model, which implies "the closing off of identity, the constriction of self-process, . . . and . . . reluctance to let in any extraneous influence."

Whether there were villains or not, there were honestly mistaken people who permitted events to occur to the detriment of the causes. Retracing four of these trends or events of recent years, then, serves a useful purpose if it leads to wisdom or resolves not to let something like them happen so simply again. Such retracing might also contribute to the eventual task of locating some boundaries and a center or core for future Christian inquiry and expression.

6

Nearsighted Leaders, Blind-Siders, and Recovery

ORGANIZATIONALISM

Problem Number One: If the mainstream religious forces are to reassume their responsibility, they will have to work with less complex organizations than they employed in the recent past. The extent of denominational and interdenominational bureaucracy became most clear to this Midwesterner during a foray to New York in the summer of 1965. Teaching there for six weeks across the street from 475 Riverside Drive, where the National Council of Churches and numerous denominations are housed, provided me with a different angle of vision from that which I had usually gained from a distance.

From a distance, I had dealt with the NCC or churchly agencies one at a time. These exposures were largely creative. No complaints: This witness is not hostile. Frequent contacts at conferences with agencies devoted to the design of church buildings, worship and the arts, communications, higher education, ministry, and the like revealed the general level of competence and dedication of the talented people in the various sectors of the Council.

Now, in New York, it would be possible to see how they interacted. They did not, for the most part. Distance had made

integration or at least perspective seem possible. The vision up
close showed that people in the building were largely unaware
of what those in the next cubicle or on another floor were doing.
The Council and the denominations resembled the modern university, "united only by a common heating plant and a common
grievance over parking."

For a number of those weeks, almost every lunch was taken
with some representative of the media, with whom I compared
notes about the state of American religion. Never before had I
conversed with such a sense of remoteness from the people
who made up the churches as I did that summer. Most of the
impressions that communicators and bureaucrats had of religious
activity, they gained from dealing with each other at such
lunches or by memoranda. Here were people at the tops of the
various pyramids communicating with each other with few of
them having much awareness of the bases.

No malign intent was behind the organization. It would be
romantic and naïve to picture that the churches can address
modern society through agencies as integrated as people think
the medieval university was. Not everything need be completely
integrated with everything else. The conservatives' alternatives
to the NCC are also intricate. "Key 73," an evangelism drive involving hundreds of churches and groups across the nation, was
born full-grown in bureaucracy and with an organizational chart
as complex as that of General Motors or the National Council
of Churches. The Southern Baptist Convention prospers despite
a heavily laden institutional overlay. A tiny, rural denomination
or congregation has as many departments as does many an ur-
banized one.

Nor are these bureaucracies always treated fairly by their
opponents. Their talents and intentions can be overlooked by
those who take one feature of their life and distort it. Thus Dr.

W. A. Criswell, pastor of First Baptist Church in Dallas—the nation's largest WASP congregation—used to criticize the World Council of Churches in Geneva for its tendencies toward becoming a superchurch. The proof was in its budget. Yet the budget of his single congregation compared favorably with the operational budget of that whole huge world-wide organization.

The complexity did help keep the Council and keeps many denominations from being responsive. In 1972 there appeared a study by Henry J. Pratt, *The Liberalization of American Protestantism*. Significantly it was subtitled *A Case Study in Complex Organizations*. When a scholar has to try to understand a church movement by reference to Amitai Etzioni's *A Comparative Analysis of Complex Organizations* rather than to some religious document, there is reason to be alert to a problem. Why should liberalization virtually be equatable with complex organizationalism?

The bureaucracies were especially unfortunate in that they ran into a decade of anti-institutionalism followed by some years of populist sentiment. The youthful rebels of the 1960s, with sound instincts if often without careful analysis, focused on Bigness as the enemy. The churches were then dismissed as part of the power structure or establishment, which enslaved people. The populists promoted the mystique of economy, grass-rootsism, accessibility, and accountability. On those terms the church leadership could be portrayed as being out of range.

Most of the vital new movements began by at least trying to extricate themselves from the Bigness models. A picture of the year in 1972 showed St. Louis' huge Pruitt-Igoe high-rise ghetto housing units being demolished by explosives. No angry militants were responsible. The authorities themselves destroyed the buildings, considering them to be impersonal and logistically ill-conceived. The modern denominational complexes were also born of that era when there had been faith in bigness and organizationalism. More recently the leaders themselves have often either quietly abandoned them or engaged in some demolition. They will not wholly succeed. In 1972 almost every major denomination, in the midst of an era of populism, personalism, and localism, spent most of its convention time on restructuring. The activity almost never meant actual simplification or cutting back.

Nowhere was organizationalism a bigger problem than in the ecumenical world. Permit a novel interpretation of early-1970s trends: I do not think the ecumenical *spirit* is in trouble. "Key 73" shows how even the right-wing moderate churches who once largely opposed ecumenism have bought its terms. They may insist that they are not compromising on basic truths, but so did the members of the earlier ecumenical movement. The terms of the relations have certainly changed when traditionalist Protestants can join in evangelizing the nation at the side of Marianist Roman Catholics. The Jesus and Pentecostal groups tend to be inter- or non-denominational. The non-denominational conservative publishing houses find the best markets. Old barriers of hostility have broken down, and people act in an ecumenical spirit even where their churches have not developed channels for them.

The complex organizationalism of ecumenism did create special difficulties. The standard symbol of a state of mind occurred at Faith and Order, a study section of the World Council of Churches, when it met in St. Andrew's, Scotland, in 1960. The church leaders were forging a statement of the terms of the unity Christians seek. The conferees came up with the assertion that "all in each place who are baptized into Jesus Christ and confess him as Lord and Savior are brought by the Holy Spirit into one fully committed fellowship." The typist who transcribed this for the press release unwittingly translated it into a revealing instance of bureaucratese: we were to come to a "full committee fellowship." In that flip of phrases is condensed much of the problem of formal ecumenism.

An informed student can take most documents of church unity and engage in a bit of detective work. He can discern which lines were written by the Methodist contributor and which by the Anglican. If he is astute, he will be able to say whether the writer was influenced by Karl Barth and attended a Continental university or whether he attended an interdenominational American school. It is often even possible to discover which committee member contributed a line. But instead of saying, "Professor So-and-So finally yielded and found an acceptable formulation," people are told, "The Methodist and the Anglican churches agreed on this point today." The analogue is to statecraft, where a Henry Kissinger accepts or drafts a formula that the American people never get to ratify (or perhaps even to see) and yet it is said, "The American position is. . . ."

Committee-drafted documents and negotiations are inevitable. They are not, however, expressive of the lived life of most church members. Understandably these members will largely ignore such resolutions. Localism takes its rise from reaction against the impersonality of such undertakings. The formal ecumenical movement was promising so long as it was threatening to someone or other. When people were being inconvenienced by it, history was being made. When it could be taken for granted, the time of promise was over.

On these terms the Consultation on Church Union never had a chance. A creative and well-intended effort to bring together over twenty million Protestants in more than ten denominations, COCU was born rich in complexity. One hundred years earlier, when the old-dominion denominations still had dominion in the WASP empire, its moves would have been ominous. People would have watched it just as in the 1960s they observed all the doings of the SDS and black organizations on the one hand or formal political agencies on the other. But the scandal of division between these denominations had ended long before the 1960s. They were not out trying to steal each other's sheep—at least not overtly. No one could complain if a few changed folds in the shuffle to suburban pastures. But proselytizing was minimal and public criticism of each other as churches was out of the question.

If the wrong student radicals or blacks got together on the wrong terms, society quaked. There might then be a burned ghetto or university building. Urban guerrillaism or upsetting demonstrations could result. But when a number of no-longer-offensive or even not-too-potent denominations spoke of coming to concord, they could awaken at best mild enthusiasm. They were more successful at arousing opposition from a few people who felt that they would be deprived of the colorful particularities enshrined in their own hymnals and polities. Few thought of COCU as an adding on of Christian benefits. It seemed to most to be a subtraction of vitalities.

Back in the 1950s, when *The Man in the Gray Flannel Suit* and *Marjorie Morningstar* vied for attention as portrayals of the safe and sane middle class in WASP and Jewish culture, someone asked rough-cut novelist Nelson Algren what he thought of both. He told them that if they were to be married on his doorstep, he doubted whether he would peek out to see what was going on. The AFL-CIO, the GOP, the NAACP, and the American Legion had too little to gain or lose from COCU to worry about one more acronym on the horizon of letterheads.

When nothing showed except the shell of a Christian unitive dream, it attracted little hope.

NCC and COCU and WCC are adaptive and may not by any means have come to demise. But their rebirth will have to be accompanied by more fluid, lighter organization and more responsiveness. That this may happen as a result of financial pinches is a good prospect. Elsewhere I have suggested that a COCU could exist as a place where symbols are pooled. Were it to catch the spirit of the pick-up-and-drop *ad hoc* ecumenism that characterizes life in the 1970s, it could do so around two slogans of American life. One is "Y'all come!" Rather than serve as an entity that suggests that everyone agrees and everything has been solved, it should simply invite people to come to it as a staging ground or arena where interaction occurs.

Then comes the second slogan: "Run up a flag and see who salutes." Life in unitive bodies would be simpler and more effective if it did not always assume that everyone every day has to relate to everyone else on the same terms on every issue. On one matter the Episcopalians and Lutherans will be close to each other—for example, in affairs liturgical. But *some* Episcopalians and *some* Lutherans will have more in common with members or agencies of other churches on other matters, including doctrine, social action, and the like. Room there may be for consensus and agreements between denominations. But it is unrealistic to picture that more consensus should appear between them than within them. The great illusion of ecumenical organizations is that there is only *an* opinion or one attitude to most subjects. It happens that the southern Presbyterians and Missouri Lutherans are among the most divided bodies in America, despite their insistence on total doctrinal agreement in ecumenical encounters. Even if there be schism in one and some breaking away in the other, what is left of either of them will never become united to any degree compatible with the myths each brings to interchurch activities.

Indifferentism will result, say those who think that committees and bureaus must first assure agreement. I prefer to speak of a "higher differentism," which can be the product of Christian people's exposures to each other, unmediated through impenetrable committees whose negotiations occur at a distance. Complex organizationalism, in other words, creates the impression that it has developed boundaries and centers, but it has succeeded only in creating illusions. Christian people, invited to come together and to respond to the symbols of their faith, will be much more likely to find boundaries and to look for the core of their traditions and terms of their life together. Let the conservative denominations and co-operative movements buy and live with the problems that the conventionally ecumenical groups are trying to overcome. They are well on their way to needing Amitai Etzioni and Henry J. Pratt to help sort out their mazes.

"GENERALS WITHOUT ARMIES"

The second of the debilitating problems came to the surface in the 1960s as a corollary or a product of the first. I call it the "generals-without-armies" syndrome, recalling this designation by a U.S. senator. After having listened to testimony by noted clerics and becoming aware of the distance between what they professed and what their clienteles back home stood for, he dismissed these leaders as being "generals without armies." If any had armies, these were out of step. Now, one kind of leader feels that being in step is *all* that matters—so he never leads. The grass-roots mystique in American religion asks for such lock-step marchers. Take a poll and find out what everyone desires, and then have the leader represent it. This is about as far from any concepts of biblical leadership as can be pictured, but it sells well.

The opposite can be called "prophetistic," as opposed to prophetic, leaderships. In this pattern the leader proudly announces that he is marching to a different drummer and the people are a priori out of step and in the wrong. He is the new seminary graduate who heads for the suburbs to preach that "one honest sermon those people ought always to have heard from my predecessor." He is the elitist who on the basis of a hard-to-duplicate set of circumstances is able to gain a perspective that more rooted and less mobile people have not been able to do. So he stands apart from them and denounces them.

Leadership calls for a different kind of pushing and pulling, wooing and chiding, winning of rapport and seeking change. The thoughtless prophetists grossly underestimated the sophistication of the other powers in the 1960s. They chose the route of denominational pronouncements on various subjects as their prime means of addressing society. Pronouncements are excellent means of addressing people in the churches, but they are less effective as representers of churchly points of view to the public.

Housing. Almost any denomination or certainly any religious social action board has somewhere along the way passed beautiful statements on the biblically based injunction to provide shelter for people. To these it adds the support of American ideals of equality and recognizes that these can be attained only through racially integrated or, at least, open housing communities. A professional advisory group prepares materials. Delegates to a national convention discuss the problem. They are men and women of good will. Whoever thinks about the problem will tend to begin to sound pretty good on an issue such as this. Rough edges of dissent at both extremes are smoothed. Eventually a resolution emerges.

It is shipped to Washington. There a congressman's secretary opens the mail and 4.2 seconds later it reposes in the wastebasket. Or the New York *Times* turns in a dutiful if brief report on this pronouncement. The story is read only by those who keep score on what goes on in social action fields. The world remains where it had been. Why? Because the congressman's secretary knows that the congressman knows how the clientele of the pronouncing denomination thinks and acts. They know that those church people are part of the problem, not the solution.

On the other hand, a black family moves into a previously unintegrated suburb. A congregation has been carefully prepared for the day by its clerical and lay leadership. Not to speak up means to acquiesce to the terror that will come: harassment of the blacks, probably the burning or bombing of their house. To speak up then means no pious pronouncement. Instead white church members move in with the blacks, suffer with them, front for them, let them alone if that is desired, welcome them to community affairs, take on all their risks. *That* represents power, produces change, however inconveniencing it may be.

In the case of selective conscientious objection, it has not been easy for the churches to find clear theological warrant for one position or another. The recent general trend has been for them to be personalistic, to look to the conscience of the one rather than the need for order on the part of many. This tradition has long roots. Many interpreters of the just-war theory have included it as a possibility. In my own associating with Protestant young objectors I have found again and again that

Martin Luther's clear support of selective objection was of value. But such defenses have not been well known.

Then the Roman Catholic bishops and a number of major Protestant bodies went on record as either encouraging or permitting selective objection to particular wars. The Congress did not cower. It knew where the majorities were in the electorate. Nor would it make so radical a move as to legitimate such objection during war times. The courts are limited in their range of action until the Congress makes explicit moves. So it was necessary for advocates of objectors to meet with draft boards and review boards, with courts and voluntary associations. Here those churchly pronouncements, designed chiefly to instruct conscience in the churches and notify outsiders of a stand, were of considerable effect.

In the cases of both housing and selective objection, someone had to be offended or scandalized by the church. It is not likely that the church can bring in new justice without inconveniencing someone or other. But how people are offended and by whom and on what terms, will tell a great deal about the rapport between the senator's churchly generals and their armies.

Failure to deal with the sophistication of the politician or unwillingness to recognize it, led some activist clerics to the point where they were not feared or opposed but simply derided. "Doesn't he know any better?" Other citizens did what they could to try to find flaws in the credentials of the activists. "You make pretty pronouncements about open housing, but I know where you S.O.B.'s live—out in the white suburbs. You advocate busing, and send your kids to a private school." There was joy in backlashdom when it was learned that Milwaukee's Father James Groppi had cached away a considerable fund as a result of his lecturing. He had not burned all his bridges to the larger society. He even held stock in the capitalistic system he was decrying. Open and frank confession of one's own complicity in the day's evils adds to credibility, just as alertness to concrete opportunities for involving people, as opposed to making pronouncements, have more telling effects. That ought to be a lesson from the 1960s.

In what preceded, a telltale trace of clericalism appeared. The attempt to tell the story of social activism in the 1960s almost always becomes the account of rabbis, priests, nuns, and ministers. Without question, on the short run the clerical garb or symbol had a shock effect. But as years passed, this effect was lessened. Instead of being a sign of visible Christian participation, it was often dismissed: "Oh, Reverend So-and-So has taken to the streets again. So what else is new?" More often, the clericalism was an indication of a failure to be effective with laity. "Reverend, you are the only member of the congregation who does not own or is not buying his own house. Let those of us who have an investment in the future here represent what it is you stand for."

What broke apart in the decade of upheaval was any sense on the part of much of the leadership for what I call precinct politics in the churches. The church is other, and more, and less than political, but because it is in the world, it is also political. Even the Jehovah's Witnesses, by *not* saluting the flag, or transfusing blood, or serving in the military, are political. There is no place to hide. But bureaucracy or organizationalism plus propheticism and pronouncement-making led many to a disregard for the precincts, the local congregations and cells.

Here again many of the social analysts and power organizers in the churches took leave of common sense by neglecting the most important base. They were always looking for "emerging viable structures of ministry," some magical new forms that would replace parish and congregation or local units. It goes without saying that local congregations are highly accidental historical developments. They are obviously not simple re-enactments of New Testament forms. They may well be supplemented or supplanted in the future. But, for now, they are where most of the religiously minded people are and where most of the power is.

The seminarians eventually came to sense this. Throughout the turmoil of the previous decade, every survey suggested that theological students and would-be professional ministers had wanted to serve everywhere but in those dour, prejudiced, low-yield congregations out there. Give them access to think tanks, community organizations, secular agencies, "emerging viable structures," boards and bureaus, and they would have power. A few years later, having learned that if they wanted to be ministers most of them would have to settle for the congregations, not a few of them began to inform their succeeding generation in the seminaries that parishes had some possibilities at least. Perhaps if the economic situation changed one day again and society allowed for the luxury of alternatives, many of them would head back in those other directions. But, in the seventies, having some sort of relation to four or five hundred adult Americans represents more opportunity than does life at the frustrating edge of underfinanced, understaffed, and misunderstood alternatives.

The glamour is still elsewhere. Foundations look with favor at less rooted, less compromised, and less compromising forms of organization. But old-pro, long-term observers are coming to the place where they have to stifle a yawn whenever they are told of a dramatic new breakthrough in ministry. Attend a gathering of the tired charismatic leaders who founded the alternative communities in the 1950s or, worse, track along behind their burdened successors, and it is likely that you will

see in these a more traditional, less malleable, less open em-
bodiment of Christianity than is present in the messiness of
congregational life. Precinct attention matters in religion as in
politics, however different their goals and purposes.

The leader in a parish/precinct gains power by serving. He
or she does not serve in order to gain power. Each situation
has its own intrinsic worth. A minister does not make a pastoral
call to the ill in order that when the person comes to health
he or she can be supportive of some program or other. A good
minister is too busy to think about such side benefits. He does
not help nurture families only so that they can help integrate a
community. A person does what the situation demands. But
situations overlap and interlock, and a caring community builds
up a treasury of concerns. The specialized organization, as an
alternative to the parish, may more focally address one issue or
another, but it also has limits. Recovery in tomorrow's religion
will be precinct based.

BLIND-SIDED FROM THE LEFT

A third event of the 1960s that helped weaken the churches
was a result of their being beguiled by the left. In football terms,
they were "blind-sided," blocked or tackled from a direction
where they were not looking and where they were unprotected.
They knew how to take care of right and center, but were
vulnerable to the left. By the left I refer to those who in that
decade called themselves "radical" or "revolutionary" in theology or practice.

Early in the decade, these churches had found themselves
progressively tied to progressive and liberal visions of the world.
Henry J. Pratt in his study of the National Council of Churches
cited four hallmarks outlined by Leslie W. Dunbar: "1) satis-
faction with the economic policies and directions of the modern

welfare state and acceptance of them as a given; 2) affirmation of America's world responsibilities and support of international cooperation; 3) the shunning of ideological or doctrinaire commitment in either economic or political matters; and 4) belief in the First, Fifth, and Fourteenth Amendments as embodiments of civil liberties essential to a free society."

The Kennedy and early Johnson administrations saw a perpetuation of those visions and commitments, and the churches tagged along and strove for relevance to them. The leadership sometimes did so at the expense of other aspects of spiritual ministry and often without being alert to the distance between them and much of the followership. This vision was often projected into the future and given some name that imparted a sense of novelty or hope: The Secular City, The Great Society, The New Frontier, and the like.

As is so often the case, the announcement of a bold new thing is often a summary statement of the dying old. No sooner were the assurances of a coming kingdom made than the nation divided into new reactionaries and a new left. The liberal forces remained statistically strong, and in some cases could and still can gather majorities. They did elect Presidents Kennedy and Johnson, the latter by an overwhelming majority, and almost elected Vice-President Humphrey to highest office, in three tests during the decade. They supported Congresses that were at least nominally to the left of President Nixon in 1968 and 1972.

The liberal case was weakening, however, in the eyes of many. The liberals were devoid of new ideas. The welfare state had become a federalized bureaucracy. World responsibility? That had produced the Vietnam War. Absence of ideology often meant absence of ideas. The support of constitutional liberties was largely nominal, and in the world of racial injustice it was usually seen to be at best partial.

According to surveys cited by Jeffrey S. Hadden in his sociological study of *The Gathering Storm in the Churches* and according to almost every alert-eyed observer and minister in the country, a gap was growing between leaders and followers. Perhaps the gulf had always been there, but reasons for its widening were growing. And the separation usually found the membership dragging its feet or protesting against religious support of the old liberal program. President Nixon began to speak of a new or silent majority of middle Americans who had had enough of most of the program. Their presence was not new to ministers and lay leaders. They were artists at living with the situation and at coping with their frustrations. Most of them knew that they had not been called to give political leadership. Few of them professed too much interest or competence. We must not picture the Catholic and Protestant leadership as being highly politically oriented. The urgency of the decade's problems drew or forced them into action.

Then came the attack on the four points from the left, including a left that announced itself as being religiously based. For that, the liberals were unprepared; hence we can speak of their being blind-sided. By the time they caught on to what was happening, the left attack had died of its own maldirection and lack of staying power.

Christian theological radicalism is certainly a legitimate rendering of the gospels. It may call the disciple to give up everything—family, parents, security, riches, academic tenure—for the sake of the announcement of the coming kingdom. It calls for bearing in one's body the wounds of Christ. Christian radicalism asks first of all what one is suffering for the cause, not how the cause can prosper. Jacques Ellul in his book on *Violence* asks would-be Christian radicals to remember a prophetic principle: Are you in a movement for the sake of the movement's goals? In effect, is your eye first on the suffering Vietnamese child or on the success of your movement and its ability to embarrass the American regime? Ellul fears the totalitarian means that are needed by the revolutionary who takes up arms, and he has no reason to trust the successful revolutionary.

Some domestic Mennonites keep the radical Christian impetus alive, as do some Latin American Catholics and an occasional black leader. But most of the people who used the banner in the 1960s never quite understood what it was all about. Rhetoric and trappings were the main features. The Jewish boy outfits himself with a yacht for Sunday afternoon on Long Island Sound. He buys the caps and maps and compasses and talks a good line. Mother: "By you, you're a sea captain; by me, you're a sea captain. By sea captains, are you a sea captain?"

When the radicals formally styled themselves as revolutionaries, confusion only grew. Several times in the sixties I can recall a presentation on stage by a self-styled Christian revolutionary who oozed *machismo*. The questions from the audience would begin. "Do you know what revolution means in the modern world?" An Arab student or a Latin American would describe the cost of revolution. "Restaurants get bombed; baby's intestines splatter over the walls. Nothing and no one is safe. Do you mean all that when you call for revolution?"

Yes. In Latin America. No. Not close to home. "I didn't really mean that when I talked about revolution." "Then, by your mother you may be a revolutionary, and by you you may be a revolutionary, but by revolutionaries you aren't a revolutionary." A *Theology Today* article ground through its little computer the writings of a number of the best-known Christian revolutionaries and could not find one who used the word as it is conventionally meant in the larger society. There are other kinds of revolutions, of course, such as the industrial revolution. And many of the circuit-riding Christian radicals backed off as soon as it became chic to do so into the call for a "cultural revolution." No one gets physically bloodied by it.

In the summer of 1969 for a moment someone acted revolutionary and bombed a mathematics center at the University of Wisconsin. A researcher was killed. When the new American revolutionaries glimpsed blood close up, they backed off.

For two or three years, whoever was not calling for top-to-bottom revolution in the name of Jesus was irrelevant to the media, the lecture circuit, the planning centers, and the seminaries. Those who would rise to the occasions with references to non-violent change, innovation, or new politics, talked into an echo chamber. A call for political involvement was square. Where have the revolutionaries gone since the late sixties? After the flirtations of the 1930s they put out post-Marxian apologies on *The God That Failed*. Now they are either saying, "I never said that," or "That's not what I meant," or "Sorry, I slightly revised my thought," or they just slink away. Even their names are hard to remember. Seminary professors on sabbatical leave along about 1968 or 1969 returned a year later to their classrooms expecting that the Christian Maoists would by then be fully in command—only to find a new generation, which wanted its hand held in smothering mothering relations.

My tone has turned unintentionally derisive. The Christian radical-revolutionary vision was not far off target. Evil did and does pervade the structures of life in all our establishments. Total repentance is needed. But most of those who spoke up for violent change did not convince their fellow Christians that they had ready alternatives. The phoenix theory never was convincing. Who would trust them to burn everything down so that from the ashes something good would come? Even the barely literate are good enough historians to know there are few precedents that would charter a willing suspension of disbelief on that scale.

As their contemporaries appraised the radicals' own style of living, they found few reasons to trust a future in their hands. Did anything they do show empathy and regard for persons? The little old lady in Cicero, Illinois, became a thing, not a person; a factor, not a soul; not part of any conceivable movement, she was expendable. What would happen to persons *after* a revolution? With an almost beautiful naïveté, the spokesmen for radicalism thought their own careers could go unexamined. But the opposition did some pop research and noticed that most of the speakers for a new age were owners of stock, tenured, with children in the better schools, happy enough to take their royalty checks, fussy about honorariums.

Theologically, the movement was marked by Manichaeanism and messianism. The Manichaean is a dualist who might as well be living in old Persia. He sees light *versus* darkness; we *versus* L.B.J.; we-whites-with-black-consciousness *versus* white institutional racism; utterly good *versus* utterly evil; good guys teamed with good God *versus* bad guys teamed with bad gods. The old Manichaeans were at least ascetic, while many of the new ones were allowed some covert hedonism.

Lest the leftovers of the radical right start sharpening their pencils to write essays on how communism infiltrated religion, let me hasten to assure them that Communists themselves were as confused by the new mixture as the American Legion would have been, had it taken pains to sort out the signals of the sixties. Symbiosis between some styles of Marxism and Christianity can be promising. But the Che-Mao-Fanon blend, laced with slogans from Herbert Marcuse and decorated with a few biblical texts, was another story entirely. Let me also notify any cultural-lag victims on the right that it would not pay them to go snooping or sleuthing for latter-day perpetuators of the revolutionary vision and tactic. They are virtually all gone.

The legacy is a benumbed and often masochistic moderate Christian left. White liberals had already become bewildered when they tooled themselves up for partnership and participation in black struggles, only to be told, "Whitey, go home!" Self-hate deepened as it began to occur to them that Vietnam was, in early stages, partly their war. When it turned out that self-styled radicals were often their own children who were rebelling against them and not against the Birchers, the generation gap led to further self-doubt about their potency. From all directions they were told that they were devoid of ideas, impotent and spent, the chief of sinners in the American community.

The Black Manifesto, to which we have already referred, illustrates the instance. James Forman was a mild revolutionary according to the terms of the 1960s. His manifesto was pre-ambled with some Marxian language. This was a good attention-getting device but hardly a charter for what his movement wanted. They wanted capital, half a billion dollars' worth of it as reparations from white churches. No one cowered, *no* one—except a few liberal-chic people. The Gallup Poll found only 2 per cent of white America ready even to entertain the idea of reparations. No doubt a smaller percentage than that would have been ready to cough up money through their churches. A board or bureau might promise to deliver here or there—but its clientele would find ways to reject the action later. Forman attacked the white liberal churches, says Henry J. Pratt, not because they had done nothing on race. Their record, he proves, was among the best—weak as it was—on this matter.

But their rhetoric led Forman to entertain the idea that they might move farther. They might be reachable. A Baptist church in a southern city, where there was money and power and little openness on racial matters, would not have been a plausible or safe target.

Jonathan's Wake caused a bit of confusion through its use of guerrilla theater at a National Council of Churches conclave in Detroit late in 1969. This was one of the last rounds for Christian radicalism in new-movement form. The movement or event involved gross miscalculation and only produced bewilderment and backlash. The Seminarians Organized for Racial Justice did a grotesque little dance on table tops at a banquet honoring Dr. Edgar Chandler, the retiring head of the Church Federation of Greater Chicago. If the National Council was weak, the Federation was powerless and comatose. Considered as an act of euthanasia, the banquet-storming might have made sense. As an act of consciousness-raising or an instrument for change, it again revealed nothing so much as the political naïveté of its planners.

A glance at the "minutes of the meeting" of Forman's group, Jonathan's Wake, or the SORJ actors makes one thing clear. There was in each little attention to the concrete sufferer, the black child in the ghetto or the bombed child in Vietnam. The obsession was largely with theatrics and thaumaturgy, the appeal was to histrionics and not to history, the concern was for the status of people in the movement and the organizational effect and not for the consequence in a coming kingdom.

A few monuments remain. Some books on *Jesus the Zealot* gather dust on publishers' remainder tables. The square, durable, and more promising sides of the movement stage occasional square, durable, and promising "Marxist-Christian dailogues," chiefly in Europe or the United States where everyone is tired.

What else is left? An occasional period piece on the religion of the revolutionaries, unsalable items on Frantz Fanon and other heroes as spiritual leaders. These are books whose manuscripts probably failed to meet publishers' deadlines and came out too late. Occasional rhetoric from the less effective corners of the Women's Liberation Movement in religion still sound revolutionary. But its spokesmen also miscalculate the power arrangements in the churches and synagogues. The real walking-wounded legacies are some religious liberals who were blind-sided from that left.

The one little billboard-sized reality about the church that the movement people overlooked (but Mennonites and Latin American Catholic radicals never forget) has to do with the nature of power in a free society. Were the civil society in the United States visibly in a prerevolutionary situation, as it is in many South American nations, radicalism-turned-revolutionary would stand some chance of having effect. It might fail, but it would do more than awaken chic responses or inspire some reportage. Why? Because civil society is coercive. No one can escape from it. Taxes are compulsory, armies are mandatory, citizenship is protected or withheld.

Religious forces, however, are voluntary. In a modern, secular, and free society no one has to belong to, attend, or support the churches. If one church offends, the member merely goes shopping for an inoffensive alternative. Clienteles can withhold consent through closed pocketbooks, inattentiveness, or the loss of the joy of participation. They know they do not even have to bother to respond to appeals. The occasional right-wing replies to Christian radicals of the 1960s were hardly noticed, ineffective, unnecessary.

Religious power resides in the depth of attachment people have and feel for shared symbols or myths that have drawn them into communities of belonging. The members of the Christian left in the 1960s traded off a spiritual capital in which they were not reinvesting. They acted as if those symbols would remain forever, even if unnurtured; that people had no place to find belonging but where they already were. The churches and synagogues were supposedly power forces that could be "used" in community organization or confrontation. They could be, only when the base of community lasted. That is why Mennonites and the Church of the Brethren take pains to feed the soul. They do so both for intrinsic reasons, because souls deserve and enjoy being fed, and for extrinsic reasons, because people who lead rich spiritual lives can be stirred to witness together. That is why Dom Helder Camara remains effective in Brazil in Catholicism, and gloomy Jacques Ellul or a William Stringfellow can at least prick some Protestant consciences. That is why James Forest of the Catholic peace movement announces that his group is going back to prayer and liturgy and meditation, and why a paroled Father Daniel Berrigan returns from prison a biblical student and teacher.

The spirit of the age in the 1970s opposes blends of religion and politics. Christians are expected to retreat into the sanctuaries of soul and experience Jesus, or to sensitivity centers and become aware of the body. But Dean Inge warned us not to let the spirit of the age set all the terms for Christians. By now they have also heard enough from Jacques Ellul and others about the danger of politicization, a pattern in which all of life is viewed as political and everything is reduced to politics. Such lessons have to sink in in the churches, but if Christian life is not wholly political, as the moderate to radical left thought it was, it is also political. Bernard Crick's defense makes sense on the whole Christian scale from running Sunday schools and parish teas to facing abortion issues and working for justice:

"Political activity is a type of moral activity; it is free activity, and it is inventive, flexible, enjoyable, and human; it can create some sense of community and yet it is not, for instance, a slave to nationalism; it does not claim to settle every problem or to make every sad heart glad, but it can help some way in nearly everything and, where it is strong, it can prevent the vast cruelties and deceits of ideological rule." Every effective pastor knows that, but few of the blind-siders of the 1960s did.

SECULAR THEOLOGY AND BOUNDARYLESSNESS

The fourth experience of the decade past from which American religionists have an opportunity to learn has to do with interpreting Christianity in the modern world. This episode has often been referred to as the time of "secular theology." Well-off conservatives never needed its way of relating to the world. Most of them worked out direct relations to it. (Recall the Texas Baptist millionaire who mingled deferred benefits *and* temporal benefits, and wanted no person to meddle with or mingle the languages about the two.) But much of the rest of American religion did take up the question of new opportunities presented by a changing world.

This is not the place for a full-scale critique of the worldly theologies of the 1960s. Only the outlines need be remembered for the present purpose, which is to see what should and can be avoided in future Christian interpretation. Thoughtful people know that something has changed since the world of primitive or medieval man or even village man in the nineteenth century. No one is quite sure what it was. In his attack on the myth of "secular man," Andrew M. Greeley joins David Martin and others of a school of thought that suggests that structural changes did occur but human nature itself remains the same and religious needs and functions are similar to what they have always been.

What changed? Natural and scientific phenomena are less likely than before to be given religious interpretations. Religion is more likely than before to be a matter of private enterprise, as people hack together for themselves more meaning systems that are less "given" than they once were. Religious forces have less power over other powers than they once did, and government, business, the military, education, and other "big" phenomena are on their own. Analysis has been born, and myth is no longer taken uncritically. That to which myth points may still be regarded as true—but people are aware that myths are myths and have to be interpreted. Religious commitment has become largely a matter of free choice. J. Milton Yinger, Will Herberg, Ernest Gellner, and others united with Greeley and Martin: We do not have simple secularization so much as we have religious change.

In theological circles, for a moment early in the 1960s, a group of thinkers took the deep and pervasive secular parts of life and made them the whole of life. This endeavor all went on in the rather rarefied atmosphere at universities and seminaries. Some of the critics have hypothesized that only there did this "secular man" ever really find a home. Theologians made projections on the basis of present trends and pictured a future given over to people who live wholly in an immanental realm, where they would be forever unmoved by the m's of meaning: metaphysics, myth, magic, mystery, mysticism, and the like.

The program varied from thinker to thinker, but some outlines are clear. The transcendental and mythical elements in the biblical materials were to be reinterpreted. The Bible's tendencies toward purging the world of sacralized politics and magical nature were accented. To discuss "God" was a problem, but Jesus belonged to history and he remained an exemplar and instigator of faith and freedom. The Church would survive largely as a community of action in the world. The Christian not only would go along grudgingly with the secular spirit of the times. He would actually be a pioneer or frontiersman in helping the world become more worldly.

Secular thought in Christianity can be seen as a half-true or half-false address to the wholeness of life. It occurred in a moment that saw what the then voguish disciples of Thomas S. Kuhn called the breakdown of models and paradigms. In such a moment there are fumbling experiments and false starts. The worldly theology thus was a complex that made a contribution to future interpretation, but it failed to reckon with too many dimensions of human experience and Christian promise to serve as the only legitimate basis of future Christian thought.

The problem once again was boundarylessness, the absence of centering. Dietrich Bonhoeffer, the German theologian who was put to death by the Nazis and whose vision of "religionless" Christianity was built on a worldly model, had pondered why he often was in communion with agnostics and distanced from nominal fellow Christians. The presuppositions, perspectives, and results of the Christian and non-Christian humanist community had virtually merged on some issues. People began to ask: Who needs the Christian route, then, with its burden of embarrassing and extraneous symbols? Can I not come to freedom better through an accessible contemporary like Albert Camus than through remote and inaccessible Jesus of Nazareth—unless special claims are made for Jesus? These claims the worldly or immanentalist thinkers were reluctant to make or defend.

The religious community, at least in America, was caught

off guard by the realization that theologians might want to innovate. Catholics in particular were used to thinking of them as defenders of the old faith, rigid antiquarians. Edmund Wilson, in reporting on *Scrolls from the Dead Sea* in 1954, tried to make the charge stick that new findings embarrassing to Christian tradition were being suppressed because Christian scholars had tried to hide difficulties from their community. No doubt many people believed him. Actually, religious scholars were coming to the point of trying to be more up to date or farther out than their colleagues. They seemed to wish to advertise a whole new theology each publishing season. After Vatican II, restraints were off Catholics and they joined their Protestant peers in the mad dash for the new.

The new was never quite new enough, however. Boundaryless and non-centered Christian thought was really a kind of tag-along or weathervane theology. First someone outside the churches had to break a path for the relevant theologian to follow. Someone else had to create a wind to which the Christian avant-garde could turn and point. Truly adventurous theology would have called into question the spirit of the time or the climate of opinion, but, for a moment, few seemed to notice that the school of worldly relevance was actually conservative. It set out to consolidate and conserve the commonly accepted notions of the time and provide them with a tardy overlay of Christian symbols.

The standard charge against the theology of the decade was that it was faddish and fickle. Scholars would completely reverse their positions from year to year, depending upon themes set by campus gurus or the approved secular authors. Such instability is natural in a time when the paradigms or models have gone and people seek new ones or when, as Robert

Jay Lifton described the Protean experience, historical continuities are broken and a flood of imagery comes from media and elsewhere. By the time of a famed Gallahue conference at Princeton in 1968, it was possible to parade threescore bestselling authors in the field of serious theology. Many of them were spending their time trying to pick up the pieces after all the tagging along and weathervaning. Devoted to the future of theology, the conference actually symbolized the end of one kind of a venture.

The whole worldly movement was based on a sense of too much confidence in the technological, political, and academic utopias that were then still in vogue. Far from being the interpretation of a "surprise-free, long-term, multifold trend," it represented reporting on a rejected way of looking at man. William Hamilton once tried to show how the old sense of wonder was disappearing from the minds of the young and gifted. He and his son looked out at the starry sky, that sky which had given Pascal and Kant and millions of others a sense of awe and mystery. "Dad, which ones did we put up there?" That which man had made to dominate nature provided the new human scale. Ten years later, when the man-in-space program spun down, the gifted inquirers in the culture were bored by the human achievement and were more likely pondering astronomy or astrology, looking back at fossils rather than ahead to space-hardware triumphs. The proclamation that Christians had not in fact been dragging their feet all those centuries in science and technology but, rather, that they had been the instigators of man's exploitation of nature was a late and new idea. It was stated just long, loud, and clear enough to be picked up a couple of years later by the ecologists, who threw it back at Christians: *You* are the people who stopped living with nature and wonder. You are thus the ecological villains!

What the impulse was that led theologians to ask, "How little must I believe in order to be considered Christian?" is hard to discern. It may have varied from person to person. Some may have been a bit insecure about their profession. One theologian told me, when it was over: "I learned that 'modern man' or 'secular man' was simply the person in whose presence I was embarrassed to admit that I was a clergyman." Maybe some of them felt left out at the margins of the academy and thought that if they tried to be like everyone else they would find acceptability. More legitimately and, one hopes, with more constancy, they knew that the old models were no longer satisfying. They were not addressing the real world in which today's Christian lived. Their program was better than their assessment of what that real world was or might become or might be willed to be.

A footnote to the worldly theology deserves to be recorded. In its various forms—as secular, radical, revolutionary, "theology of future and hope," "theology of play," or "political theology"—it was almost always designed for the young and healthy, the middle-class and mobile. Dietrich Bonhoeffer had scolded Christians for ministering only to the few who were anxious, neurotic, intellectual, existential, the "secularized Methodists." He wanted men addressed by the gospel in the situations of human health and wealth. Most of the human race never was and remains a long way from becoming free on the terms of Western academic theologians' models.

Monika Konrad Hellwig, in an almost unnoticeable corner of *Cross Currents* in 1972, asked it well: "What do I say to a friend who is dying of cancer, beyond my silent presence? We are curiously short of the poetry of hope that has relevance to that context. What are we offering the celibate who has not begotten his own stakes in the history of the future? We presently lack the symbols of this ancient and constant Christian conviction. Most of all, where is the revolutionary to look for motivation to give the necessary utterance of hope when he is asked to face premature death that others may live? The praxis out of which a theology of revolution can forge itself is a living tradition of radical self-sacrifice. It must be admitted that the myths that support this have been attenuated for lack of telling."

Her verdict: "Where theology has been is with the young, the healthy, the married, the activist, the laity. In asking where it must go from here, we are compelled to take into account that no matter what the future of the world, all men are threatened with old age, ill health and widowhood, and, inexorably, all face death." Tomorrow's theology will have to address these situations too.

The culture took its turn, and with it theologians' weathervanes turned. Some simply accepted the new culturally available models of newly religious man, and spoke with ease again of transcendence, mystery, and myth. When the scholars only provided a gloss for what people already knew or saw, they were as dismissible and disposable as their predecessors had been in the mid-sixties. The world of theology, as a result, had become curiously if temporarily diminished.

The bureaucrats, generals without armies, radicals, and secular Christian thinkers came on the scene in a time when "wise men hoped." Some of them *were* wise. But the scene and circumstances changed, and tomorrow's religious forces have little to gain by repeating the mistakes to which these predeces-

sors were doomed, any more than they would profit from following those who never ventured and never risked.

AUTOMATIC TRANSMISSION OF FAITH

A survey of what went wrong deserves to be balanced by
some projections of what could go right. The quest for the immediate experience of Jesus or the Spirit has not been the only
new accent in the religion of the American churches in the
early 1970s. A whole series of adjustments or changes in
emphasis began to appear in reaction to trends from the recent
past. Enthusiasm for churchly social action, for large-scale ethical
concern, and for conventional organizational ecumenism waned,
but church religion did not disappear. Signs of recovery are present.

The one word that best characterizes the emerging phase is
"intention." Tomorrow's Christianity will be more intentional
and purposive than recent religion has been. Willem Hendrick
van de Pol once wrote a book called *The End of Conventional
Christianity*. If by "conventional" is meant a resort to old patterns, his prophecy was wrong. But if we think of "conventional" as "automatically transmitted," his point is appropriate.
For centuries, a believer simply inherited the parental faith and
either intensified it or let it wane; the range of other choices was
usually quite small. The New England farm boy could not easily have entertained Zen Buddhism, and the southern rural
black did not have available to him the literary ties that make
black African religion a possibility for his grandson.

Mobility enables people to be disengaged from a tradition.
Mass higher education allows young people to "make a break."
The weakening of religious educational agencies and of the
family as a teaching center means that many of the gestures and
postures, the nuances and doctrines of the past are not routinely

handed on. The last generation in which "conventional" Christianity is simply inherited is passing.

INTENTIONAL CHRISTIANITY

Tomorrow's Christian will be one because he or she has a project, an intention. The Christian person will be able to articulate the features of his personal quest. For some it will be a search for a stable identity. I know who I am when I am found in Christ or in the pew of the First Baptist Church. For others it may be a theological intention, however informally expressed. I find that life takes on meaning when Jesus Christ takes over; He is "the answer." Still others express a liturgical intention: adhering to the church year or to the rhythms of the week and the day provides a pattern of meaning and is a bearer of hope. Maybe another Christian will find ethical outlets, or aesthetic possibilities. Very practical matters can be addressed. I overcome loneliness by being accepted. Church provides an occasion for expressing my ego. I get to run something, or am important to someone. This is not to say that talk about divine initiative disappears, or that the sense of being grasped by grace is gone. But such talk and sense appear in a different context when I have many other choices than when I am programmed to express myself only within one tradition about which no one ever asked questions.

Intentional Christianity will inevitably call for gathering of people around intentions. Jesus people look up other Jesus people. Pentecostals tend to distance themselves from all others except Pentecostals. Advocates of mod liturgies find each other. Christian sensitivity-training devotees are attracted chiefly to the like-minded or, should one say, to those who "feel" similarly. The hazards of elitism and new sectarianism, of faddism and novelty seeking are obvious. The "great big messy church," which has usually provided support, may seem remote from new proclivities.

Automatic Christianity will normally appear to have more weight and power than intentional Christianity does. It tends to be coextensive with the culture. Everyone who does not take pains to be a dissenter is numbered among the believers. True, the majority of Americans for decades to come may identify themselves as Protestant, Catholic, or Jew to the pollster, but the percentage of those who may potentially be mobilized around those inherited causes will probably be considerably smaller than in the past.

Some measure of decline in the numbers of automatic Christians was present all through the 1960s, not in the sense of the absolute lessening of numbers but in the failure of churches to continue to gain over against general population trends. The controversial stands taken by many churches during that decade could not help but lead to some reaction. More important as a source of decline was the subtler secularization that went with changes of practice. The long weekend, for instance, kept people from their home places of worship. Their spiritual life tended to be "nickeled and dimed" to death because new patterns provided no occasions for developing that life.

In America, size matters. This is a curious feature in the case of a faith born in the midst of threes and twelves and chartered by one who had a universal vision but who counted the cost of discipleship as being more indicative of devotion than numbers of followers. If the lines on the graphs do not go up in American churchdom, panic or depression sets in. One difficulty the current leadership has in coming to terms with declines is the fact that it came to power during the 1950s, the most artificial decade in American religious history. From the 1770s through the 1950s, it is true, affiliation and support for churches continued to grow very gradually. But in the 1950s the postwar generation settled down into the suburban churches, built and paid for them, erected college chapels, and made churchgoing "the thing to do." Few look back on that period as a time of enriching spirituality or ennobling ethics in religion. People found relatively easy answers to their searches.

Those whose vision of leadership was shaped in the 1920s through the 1940s or again in the 1960s do not have the same sense of loss. But the leaders who see declines will reach out for anything that promises new growth; if the Jesus movement or Pentecostalism or the new sectarianism promises something for the expansion in quantity of the churches, leaders will exploit it. So the relative purity of intentional Christianity is compromised by the newer passion for mere growth, and much of the religious plot in the immediate future will represent agonizing over the tension.

SPIRITUAL EXPRESSION AND PERSONALISM

Accompanying the intentional trend is a second one, toward spiritual expression. This has been implied throughout the discussion of the new enthusiasm, but it is applicable also in quieter circles of Christianity. Merely secular or worldly Christianity was unsatisfying. People called again for an appeal to the transcendent. Devotionalism replaced ethicism; "soul" found its place. This trend was present across the spectrum of denominations, from the prospering through the starving. Overly programmed Christianity was rejected. Those who wanted to be Christian wanted to be so in order to escape some of the computerized pressures, and they did not welcome these in religion.

Much of this new spirituality took form in the personalism that people identified with their religious hopes. With a book called *The Age of the Person* (*Das personale Zeitalter*) in

Germany in 1960, Dietrich von Oppen would seem to have been wide of the mark. Orwellian and Wellsian or Kafkaesque visions of an impersonal or depersonalizing world predominated. By the time of the English translation in 1969, Von Oppen's concern began to make sense. The world of organizations still threatened. Objectivism, totalitarianism, and business hierarchies impinged on man. But, argued Von Oppen, some zones of life still offered refuge and freedom. The family could be one of these; so could the cells or congregations of the church.

Bureaucracy became the mistrusted word in subsequent religion. It did not disappear, but faith in it was shaken. Remote boards and committees, whether in Rome or Geneva, at 475 Riverside Drive in New York or at denominational headquarters, were dismissed or rejected. Economic problems associated with inflation and recession and some passive or active withholding of funds for bureaucracies on the part of the faithful coincidentally played a part in cutting down the size and power of organizational Christianity.

Over against bureaucratic Christianity there developed a sometimes naïve personalism, in which religious hopes were reposed in what Sam Keen called "the soft revolution." Thomas Oden spoke of "the new pietism," when he noted how a calculated interpersonalism as taken up by the churches filled the old void in life to which pietism and early Methodism had addressed themselves. I refer to the attention given by many Christians to the various cults of group therapy, transactional analysis, sensitivity training, body affirmation, witnessing-and-confessing engagements, encounter groups, and other versions of what Oden calls "the intensive group experience."

A mystical faith resides in the small group. Here again practical exigency may have played its part. A friend in campus ministry asks for all the books one can find about small groups.

"Small groups are all that I ever see." But, for others, the small-group experience has helped assure a personal grasp of the faith and an enhancement of Christian life. One Episcopal theologian contends that there is not a priest in his diocese who had not seen all the terms on which he entered ministry undercut. The earlier theology, liturgy, status system, and the ethical and organizational patterns have disappeared. Hardly one of these priests can resist the temptation to make the small-group experience the whole show, the complete shape of his ministry. The cultic development of personhood, an exaggeration of a classic Christian theme, is not confined to the suffering denominations. The prospering ones have welcomed Jesus and Pentecostal accents in part because of what they contribute to the new personalism.

From one point of view, it is legitimate to hope that the personalist strand will remain. Most of the time, most of the pressures of late-twentieth-century life will be anti-personal. A crowding and ever more complex world will be given to machines and media manipulation as never before, and if religion can be a center of refuge or a counterforce, that will be all to the good. The religious leadership is likely to find fulfillment in such a time. Seminarians anticipated the change, and many of them even deserted the social accent that had so deeply moved their older brothers and sisters. My own occasional and tangential contacts with future professional ministers confirm what is reported on all hands. Whereas throughout the 1960s a faculty constantly had to remind students that religion had a personal dimension, I woke up to the altered circumstance in the fall of 1971 as a coteacher of a course on orientation to ministry.

The setting was an ecumenical divinity school in a university that is pluralistic and secular in basis. Ministry students there normally represent an advance guard and are interested in experiment and innovation. As a course assignment, nine students were to write something on a problem of ministry to which they would like to address themselves, or project a vision of ministry attractive to them. On eight of the nine corrected papers it was necessary to add a note to this effect: "Remember, Christianity has not only personal but also social dimensions."

Some seminaries may retool and cater entirely to the new personalism in a quest for relevance. Fulfilled ministry will have to take into account both the individual and social, personal-private and public sides of Christian life. But, for the fad followers, the pendulum has swung. Seminary recruiting literature through much of the 1960s portrayed almost fictitious possibilities for ministry. The men and women pictured were usually in the forefront of some sort of public activity. The pictures in the 1970s are more honest, because personal ministries have always been available: bedside pastoral work, cellular activity, and the like. But they can be overstressed.

PEOPLEHOOD IN THE FUTURE

Intentional Christianity, born of both the new accent on experience and of a new cultural situation, will express itself in purposive, spiritual, and personal forms as opposed to accidental, programmatic, or bureaucratic fashions. A second major projection for tomorrow's Christianity is that it will be more "popular" than in the past. By popular I do not necessarily mean better liked or more vulgar or more widespread or merely prevailing, as the dictionary does. If only the new English noun "peoplehood" had an adjective, it would be appropriate. "Peoplehoody," fortunately, sounds so bizarre that all temptations to use it are easy to resist, and one need only keep in mind the special meaning of "popular" in this argument.

Tomorrow's Christianity will be more preoccupied with the roots and character of the people who make it up. This is another corollary of the anti-institutionalism that marks present-day renewal efforts. The new popularism makes no secret of the racial, ethnic, generational, or gendered grounds for life as part of "the People of God." The Second Vatican Council chose the "people" metaphor as its favorite, as a reminder of the character of Christianity and as a judgment against institutionalism or against static and deadening images of the Church.

This particularism is a kind of problem for ecumenical Christianity. By definition, the Church is one, both in its origin and in its final goal. While one of these belongs irretrievably to the past and the other may not appear inside history—the Church is always in the process of giving evidence of the unity it is experiencing and finding—the unitive note cannot be forgotten. But when the hoped-for unity began to be realized chiefly by committees, in documents, through boards and bureaus which were not expressive of popular life, reaction or boredom set in. No one wanted the homogenized polity or liturgy they feared would be forthcoming from Rome or Geneva or New York. Ecumenical hymnals were informative and enriching, and few Christians have failed to profit from exposure through them to other traditions.

The tendency, however, has been to be eclectic and bland. Committee concoctions rarely preserve the gut and maw of the particular styles. Blacks find only their most serene and soul-less spirituals transmitted to whites; Southern Baptists locate only the more sentimental and sugary of their soul songs in books that impart the gospel tradition to non-Baptists; Lutherans find a couple of familiar and easy-to-sing chorales in the homogenized hymnals, but those *Ur*-chorales, primitive and elemental, necessarily disappear. Preaching styles are monotoned, Christian art becomes monochromatic, organizational charts monotonous.

The attempts to manifest a sense of power and identity in the black movement in Christianity have inspired others to be more particularistic. Black religion or black theology has contributed richly to ecumenical faith, even though some of its spokesmen have been separatistic and unwilling to subject their expression of the norms of a divine judgment. Before long, Latin American and Chicano Catholics began to recover or make better known a pride in their special forms of grasping the faith. Christian American Indians no longer felt it necessary to hide their native religious contributions and fusions. Roman Catholic ethnic or national churches, having been buffeted by the homogenizers and glossier types, were free to assert that they, too, had valid and distinctive grasps of Christianity. Even some cowering WASPs came out from cover and suggested that not everything had been bad in the tradition that provided the floor for everyone else's self-esteem.

Particularism is a penultimate, not an ultimate expression of Christianity. It represents troubles just as it embodies hope. It will take different forms in different ages. In the nineteenth century, denominations were sufficiently defined that they could perform the task of providing identity and power. By the middle of the twentieth century, sociologists such as Will Herberg and Gerhard Lenski were finding that three or four pools of resource and history, Protestant (white/black), Catholic, and Jew served. In the 1970s, race and ethnicity served for many. That may all pass in the grinding up and mixing processes of American life, though it passes more slowly than most had thought. What we are learning again is that just as people are not humans in general, they are also not Christians in general. Before the ultimate unity is realized, they have scurried back and dug in and begun to enjoy a mesh of particular bases in various senses of "peoplehood."

Popular Christianity will also in some respects be more lay oriented, though I am more reluctant to project the degree to which this will be true. Some romantics have suggested that tomorrow's faith will be propagated almost entirely by non-professionals, people who have not undergone some special kind of ordination. The reasons for these suggestions are many and obvious. During the sixties some anti-clericalism appeared. People who resented Father James Groppi and the Berrigans, Martin Luther King and Chaplain William S. Coffin projected their mistrust or rage on a whole caste. After Vatican II, Roman Catholics could feel that they were opposing their bishop without opposing God. Some of the old mystique was gone. Being a cleric did not provide the protected state it once had.

A second reason for such projection lay in the economic future of the church. While there would be many prosperous sectors, it was clear that one could not foresee four decades ahead—the span of a ministry—the survival of all the forms on which the bulk of ministry relies for support. Seminary enrollments in Protestantism, for example, held their own in the 1960s. But the number of pulpits declined moderately and the number of non-parochial ministries dropped drastically. Suddenly there was a temporary pastoral oversupply. The expense of maintaining complex modern ministries leads some to hold back and urge that more ministers should be tentmakers, as was St. Paul, or worker-priests, on the French model.

Ideology plays a role too. Popular Christianity propagates the mystique of acceptance and involvement. It would affirm the ministry and the gifts of all of Christ's people. A professional clergy complicates matters, hints at organizationalism, may divide Christians into different strata of status, and may deper-

sonalize the spiritual quest. So goes the argument. Some, therefore, particularly in radical Catholicism, began to advocate a
kind of priestless church.

While there will no doubt be a cutback in the number of full-
time ordained and professional men and women in ministry, it
is hard to picture the disappearance of a clergy. In a technical
world, "what is everybody's job is nobody's job," and it will be
difficult for Christian cells to keep a full ministry before them
without someone set aside for the task. The sanctions may
change, but the sanctioning will likely go on. Perhaps churches
will alter greatly their requirements for ordination, but some
kind of ordaining will probably persist. The mystique more
than the numbers will have changed.

THE LOCAL REALITY

Finally, popular-particular-lay Christianity will continue to
accent the local. On the face of it, this also seems to be a para-
doxical if not absurd direction for churches to take. Just as
"spaceship earth" or "the global village" can at last conceive
of united Christianity while Christians reparticularize, so that
complex world demands and allows for a symbolic network of
expression that can reach all sorts and conditions of people.
The localized faith cannot. It is vulnerable to all the tendencies
of myopia, self-congratulation, and prejudice to which local en-
tities are always exposed. But local-centered Christianity is on
the rise and will probably continue to find its place.

The local is the locale for "the age of the person." People
who share a religious vision have to test it, speak about it, bear
one another's burdens. Grand-scale and mass Christianity did
not allow for this. For good and bad reasons, people want to
make decisions—especially about budgets and leadership—without outside interference. They want to be in control of some-

thing that affects their lives, and if government, business, and education are ever-more-remote conglomerates, they will seek in religion a responsive reality.

The popular Christianity described and projected here has good New Testament warrant. The charter documents of Christianity are highly conscious of Jew and Greek, Asian and European, Ephesian and Jerusalemite. They recognize the contributions of rabbis and poets, apostles and obviously lay people. They show that the local circumstances impart a flavor to each cell or congregation. Tomorrow's Christian can accent that side and be in the tradition; he will also have to listen to the ways in which each of these is also judged and transcended in this faith. People who seek a continuing city will not find too much sustenance in their passing local villages. A faith that overcomes differences between Jew and Greek cannot be content to let black or white, American or European theology pre-empt the field or be out of contact with each other.

7

We Are Condemned to Meaning

HELP FROM THE SHIPWRECKED

"The sense of being shipwrecked, since it is the truth about life, already means a measure of rescue. I therefore believe only in the thoughts of the shipwrecked." José Ortega y Gasset would not have paid much attention to the thought of those who always felt secure because their ship had ever more ballast. The self-confident illusionists who think that all is well for the future of religion and a humane society because for a moment they can advertise a Christian revival, would not have impressed him. But those who are aware of the depth of crisis in a time when the condition of being numbed is part of the crisis, would be more credible. I have tried to collate some of the expressions about signs of vitality from those who are thus aware. To pick up the Ortegan metaphor: they have reached the lifeboats and now and then even have a land-sighting.

Without some quickening of morale it is not likely that a turn can be taken. Some occasions for such a lift have appeared. Not everyone is content with the situation of stability and stasis that goes with the act of adding ever more ballast. Behind my writing is the assumption that people and culture in the foreseeable future will not be purely secular, given to the models either of secular man or secular culture. People, or at least many of them, will be somehow religious, somehow given to finding meaning and ultimate values. Many will somehow come together around stories and symbols to engage in rites and to give expression to their vision.

Second, I assume that in Western culture and in the United States much of their expression will continue to pick up from Jewish-Christian or biblical themes and traditions. These are deeply bonded with their history. However much they are neglected or attenuated, renewals of religious concern will somehow force significant numbers of people to come to terms with their own lore. The turning during the past decade first from a preoccupation with the secular to the religious and then to the Jewish and Christian is not a surprising turn of events to those who recognize how searches for identity and power are rooted in long histories.

The more interesting questions for the future have to do with how some people will be religious and how they will be Christian. In the recent past the sense of adventure was min-imized as people sought safe and secure experiences for them-selves. But ballasting is finally self-defeating. Eventually those who add too much weight find that the balloons cannot fly at all and the ships cannot move. They then jettison some of the weight for the sake of motion. Something other than an indom-itable optimism—mine is very domitable, and I "remain, never-theless, cautiously pessimistic"—moves me to tabulate and point to some of the signs of motion and life.

THE FIRE OF NEW CONSCIOUSNESS

For a beginning, we can recall and organize some signals of a turn to a new consciousness that have already been alluded to casually. They are related to different ways of conceiving peoplehood and particularity. The first of these has to do with the new recognition of the role of women and the sense of sisterhood that marks and will continue to mark religious responses. Movements rise and crest, come and go, and it would be hazardous to predict the degree of success one or another of the forms of the women's liberation movements will have. They can experience backlash or entropy, or may have new surges. But even if nothing new occurs, enough change has already appeared to assure different futures.

The change is noticeable in habits of speech, in now-automatic new ways of thinking about women's status and potential. Women who were once diffident about self-assertion became more open and bold, and were not likely to revert to old ways, also in the religious field. The path to full recognition, symbolized by the ordination of women in churches like the Roman Catholic, where this has not previously occurred, may be long, twisted, and devious. But there is a path, and there are other symbols. The opponents seem to be on the defensive.

The liberation of women may be a more hopeful sign of Christian renewal than are the statistics of religious awakening. Fresh potential is evident when people take a new angle of vision to see their history. For people to have perspective on the role of the Christian majority, and in the laity we can assume that women do have that majority, they have taken a whole new run at their history. The Bible has to be reread, every turn in the history and the tradition has to be reappraised, conventional habits of thinking have to be turned around. New sources of power are available during and from such a retracing.

A second alteration of ways of looking at the world has come with the movements of black identity and power. In the early 1960s much of the Christian recovery of an ethical note was associated with Martin Luther King. In the later 1960s some of the few creative stirrings in theology came from racially conscious "black theologians." So in the early 1970s black participants in evangelical causes—the Bill Pannells and Tom Skinners —better than others have reminded the soul-winners that Christianity has to do with whole persons and whole causes. These black leaders may not represent intoxicating revolutionism to the thrill seekers. They do stand for more than the act of adding weight to a security-seeking society.

Just as a change in consciousness has not brought women to complete fulfillment and freedom, so the new ways of thinking and looking induced by the black movement have not brought full justice. However, the movement has come to the point where both black and non-black Americans "can't go home again" to those old psychic furnished apartments where they lived in the days of slavery and segregation or subjugation.

The blacks have taught other Christians something of what it is to respond as a people to the call of a word of God. Nonblacks have learned something of a sense of happening and movement from a people that is experiencing liberation. While earlier the movement often represented only shock and threat to those who had not had a part in it, the novelty and jolt have worn away now, and permanent contributions can result. Blacks and other neglected or suppressed races, by exposing their histories to view, have revealed to the American majority something of a tragic sense that success-minded Christians had lacked. They have produced for view and sharing a record of suffering or of bearing the wounds of Christ that challenges the complacent. Out of their touch with Africa they have brought to the heart of American religion different modes of looking at nature and spirit. From their long isolation in America they have developed particular styles of worship and song, and have made these available for other Christians.

As in the case of liberated women, assertive blacks have occasioned a rereading of the record of Christianity. People seldom are swept up by the power of the Bible or the church's past if they merely accept these routinely and read the record without looking for something in particular. The particular looking nowadays often has to do with questions such as "What is a 'people,' in this lineage?" "How does suffering turn to triumph?" "What does the experience of freedom in Christ mean to people?" Black self-consciousness offers intrinsic worth for blacks. It has a marked effect on the characteristic ways of thinking on the part of non-blacks, including those who are resistant or who would not even grudgingly be able yet to send a card of thanks.

The third popular ("peoplehood") source of new vitality has come, particularly to Catholicism, through the fresh sense of ethnicity. I do not refer here to voguish identifications on the part of a few intellectuals with hardhats and silent majoritarians. One seldom finds a member of these ethnic groups who is conscious that he or she has a new spokesman or deputy. Nor is this the time to forget the powers of assimilation and mixing or melting that the pluralist process has in store for ethnic groups in the future. It does not mean that Italian Power, Polish Power, or Serbo-Croatian Power is by nature a healthy assertion for the church ecumenical or that America has room for Christian Balkanization and new fragmentation.

The ethnic consciousness, however, has come along far enough that a whole sector of American life that had once been dismissed as ballast and dead weight is now regarded as a force to be reckoned with, as a people of promise. The elitism of WASP and Jewish America—which came to be linked with the elitism of black leadership—has been checked by the aggressive recovery of a sense of power and identity among Catholic and

Protestant "minorities," minorities that, taken together, make up the majority. As their particular histories are being re-explored, more of the catholicity of the church can be exposed to view, more varieties in the tradition can be apparent.

That word about the elitism of WASPs having been compromised may lead someone to think that here is another instance of White Anglo-Saxon Protestants and their kith serving once more as the neutral background for colorful movements, the bland reference point for excitements. However, women, blacks, Indians, youth, Chicanos, Jews, and other movement people(s) have served to stimulate change among the old majority as well. The first reaction was backlash, followed by guilt and self-hate, the worst possible emotions for a group to hold if it is to be of any use to others in the world. But as the white Protestants of Anglo background took a second glance and recognized both their minority status and their special contribution to American religious history in their majority years, they began to see how necessary a rereading of the record also was for them. If that first review led to the exposure to view of ugly strands, a second look showed how they had been custodians of a word about the promise of American life and still were responsive to that word and promise.

The result of these recoveries could be a new tribalism that could set back life in the body of Christ. More likely it will represent a new patterning of subcommunities, on the model of denominations in the ecumenical age. But tribalism has its creative side too, and the color and community it offers can take the churches out of their bland condition more than will renewed sectarianism.

THE LOCAL PRECINCTS

A second locale for pointing to peoplehood, after the canvass of racial, ethnic, and other movements, is the local Christian congregation. However unfashionable the topic may have been for the past three decades, one basic point keeps coming back. If the precincts are healthy, the church's body politic can become healthy. If they are in bad condition, the whole suffers. Recoveries of morale may not begin there, but unless it occurs also in the parishes and local churches, intellectuals and social analysts will have little to talk about except ephemeral non-parochial experiments or hoped-for new forms.

Ministerial morale has been a problem through the years after the institutional revival of the 1950s. However soul-less that decade's religion might have been, spiritual poverty could be covered over then because there were so many success stories. Church building neared the one billion dollar mark annually, and the leadership of such building parishes had a visible sign of achievement on their hands. The suburban flight made possible the growth of local congregations, for this move was one of the great migrations of modern history. By the end of the 1960s the suburbs housed the American majority, and they were safely churched.

The sixties found curiosity turning elsewhere. Civil rights, social activism, the Vatican Council, death-of-God theology, Jesus and Pentecostal movements all distracted from the local scene, and the drama was largely gone. For a time in the late years of the decade the press was full of stories about ministers who were leaving their pulpits or despairing in them. Whether or not the flow through the back sacristy door has continued, one hears less about it today. For one thing, the "morale gap" between clergy and other professions closed simply because other professions were in similar trouble. The academic world's market tightened, creating new insecurities. Then the business world was in trouble, and many mid-career executives found themselves in search of new jobs.

On the more positive side, cultural changes toward a new personalism, localism, and concern for intimacy brought the fields of ministerial expertise to the fore again. The disappearance of so many experimental ministries and the economic pinch that caused a cutback in the world of bureaus and boards left the local pastoral minister standing on his own Monadnock, like some sort of survivor.

The role seldom brought glamour, but it more frequently now brought meaning. The cleric was no longer an irrelevant sideliner. He had access to the once-despised middle American; priests knew that their "ethnic" parishioners were being wooed by the politicians. Protestant ministers learned that their members, black and white, held balances of power in the dynamics of the modern civil society. This did not mean that the pastors plunged into new political life. They could, however, make the case that the health and outlook of the people to whom they ministered were of more consequence than either the observers of mass society or those who believed that only elites made history would ever have allowed.

For a time early in the seventies I clipped newspaper interviews with the leadership of declining churches, whether in West Germany or Chicago's suburbs. Reporter after reporter heard the same story: slight declines in the quantity of church membership were balanced by increases in quality. Not only the worn-down pillars remained to hold the structure up. Those who remained included the dedicated, those who had weathered the overadvertised claims of booming 1950s-style religion and the buffeting of the 1960s. A great sifting had occurred, and those who remained could be counted on more than before. If it is true that the decline bottomed out and stabilized, as some claim it did, or if new growth in the "new dominion" denominations spreads a bit farther, I will have to start a new file. Will those same ministers admit that quality controls are harder to maintain as the numbers at the fringes grow again?

The question of health in the parishes does not simply follow the pattern of growth. Many a minister of a parish typed as "mainline" and, hence, presumably suffering from decline, will say, in effect: "There's a lot going on out there. The ecumenical and denominational forces do not know quite how to summon it, and the media miss the story. But people have 'come through' in amazing if quiet ways. Loyalty and dedication show up in surprising ways." These reports seem to counter the cynicism one heard when the ministers' main vision was one of congregational resistance to social change. These accounts are still being made at a time when the leaders are far from satisfied with their peoples' response to the biblical prophetic note.

The paradox of the 1960s was that those who did not have power in the churches used it; those who did have power did not use it. Unrepresentative "generals without armies" and religious revolutionaries without followings knew well the rhetoric that created the illusion of power. The world was little changed. The local congregations—where turns to a humane society, a more just order, and a richer cultural expression were possibilities—remained silent. The true power situation is now being exposed to view. If less dramatic, it still holds potency.

So we are back to the congregations. This motif has not changed from my periodic earlier reports in 1959, 1963, and 1969. From the beginning, this attention to the precincts in the church's order has sometimes been termed "morphological fundamentalism," and each time it seems worthwhile to reckon with that charge. Everyone knows we are in a cultural revolution, rich in possibilities for epochal change. Anyone who has a head to use should know that local congregations are adapted to the old order that is passing but will be dysfunctional in the new. Why not dismiss them? From the beginning, the alternatives—experimental communities—have been advertised as richer in promise. Is there, then, some romanticism marking my approach?

Hardly. The uncritical defenders of these precincts have just as consistently been irritated not over morphological fundamentalism or contentment with existing forms and the rigid defense of them, but over the criticism that these congregations have needed and received. They are not in simple continuity with the biblical pictures of Christian community. Microcosmic in their embodiments of human hopes and fears, they cannot be miniature representatives of all that the church is to be and do in the world. They are by nature parochial (parish= *parochia*) and provincial, captive of time and place, given to temptations of self-importance and the hazards of prejudice. Survival interests will limit their capability for sacrifice. So much of what most of them do is simply beside the point and boring. One hardly needs to repeat that message, however. The time to toss a few stones through the stained glass, to let some air in, occurred when they were fat and prosperous, in the 1950s. A decade later, when they had been blasted and remained as hulks, it was time to engage in some restoring.

The cultural-revolution thesis is persuasive. Should it ever fully occur, it is not likely that the congregations we now have will have survived. The stresses and strains of the long weekend, for example, are beginning to show even where people have deep and basic loyalties. The leadership tries to adapt. If people are not around from Friday night through Sunday night, America's conventional times for worship, give them what they need, it is reasoned. Golfers' special services on Thursday night or fishermen's specials on Tuesday—these will attract. The first week, a couple of dozen people show up. A month later, dwindling has occurred. By the end of the season the staff out-numbers the worshipers. People then lapse back and lose heart, knowing that the opportunities for gathering the group have diminished. Illustrations could be multiplied. The theme rein-forces the formula: we are too far into the cultural revolution to make the old forms really effective, but not far enough through it for the new forms to have emerged.

PARA-CONGREGATIONS

In the meantime, then, it is in the self-interest of conventional parishioners to encourage pioneers who are trying to lead to the emergence. For the most part, during the past quarter century, these have appeared in middle-class America, and have drawn on the discontented and restless membership of the existing churches. Experimental congregations in suburbia have often been perceived as a threat. Their clienteles are usually highly educated, reasonably mobile souls who would probably be classi-fied as dropouts from existing parishes. Theirs are usually rather zesty and joyful gatherings, free to take up new challenges. Their members are as committed as are their counterparts in conservative sects.

While the total number of communicants in these para-congregations may very well number at best in the thousands over against one hundred million regulars, many of the regulars have been unable to share their victories with joy or to mourn in their defeats. The loss of a few congregations to them at first seems unnerving. Some show envy at the excitements in their new forms. Certainly there is some restlessness over the chal-lenges the fresh communities offer to the complacent. But in catholic Christianity they have to be tolerated as part of the search for new models or paradigms. More than tolerated, they have to be looked to for expressions that cannot be initiated in routine parishes.

From these para-congregations it is possible to project the one major change in character that should stand out above all others on the agenda. If tomorrow's Christianity will be intentional and not automatic and conventional, parochial life will have to give expression to a variety of intentions. Small groups will almost inevitably play a part in that future; what these small groups are to do and to be is the urgent issue. The anonymity and anomie of the large parish unit is often broken down only to cater to the desires for personal recognition among people.

The small groups, however, can supplement each other by offering different intentional outlets and projects. Both singles and couples, the young and the old, regathered in congregations around projects and not around accidents of age and gender, can focus annually on different intentions. The personnel of the cells could constantly be shuffled to prevent in-group life and elitism. One cell could take on the problems of aging in the local community. Another might tackle a theological issue. A third might probe the question of values in the schools, while the next one works on the drug culture. Another might give expression to liturgical or literary interests, while one more might try to be a window on the larger world of the Biafras and Bangladeshes. They all would come together frequently, as at weekly worship, because they would each be carrying more burden than they should and would be more focused than their whole spiritual health will tolerate. But the common life would be vivified by the particular accents. Rather than representing utopian dreaming, these two paragraphs merely report on impressions gained from those congregations that seem to be most alive and open.

Implied throughout in the withholding of simple consent to the self-contained congregational model is a recognition that what is often called "the new localism" brings a whole new set of problems. Chief among these is what might be called the matter of the symbolic network. No local unit is or can fairly represent a cross section of the human or Christian family. Despite the best efforts of metropolitan people to bring pluralism of race, ethnic group, social class, and economic levels into a church, there is rarely much of a distribution. Empathy for others in a metropolis is hard to come by, and real regard for the people of most of the world will be lacking. The Christian church in its catholicity would demand and offer such a vision of variety. Huddled together in local units, Christians often lose interest in the sorts and conditions of men. New attentiveness to mass media, travel, reportage, shared experience, and ecumenism will be called for. But at least the survival of the local units has provided a base from which the question of the symbolic network can be entertained.

SOUL AND SPIRIT

New people and surviving congregations are the first two signs of vitality. A third "lighting of the fire" relates to the question of "soul," the reinstatement of concerns for the spiritual that have marked Christian and Jewish life in most recent years. While the most noticed version of the Jesus and Pentecostal movements may hold little long-range promise, they are welcome as signs of the appeal of religious experience and point to often overlooked dimensions of man. This is not to say that neither has anything intrinsic to offer. Rather, both causes have enough advocates already and do not need a minor advertisement here. What will likely prove durable about both, especially as they make or keep a place in what is often called "mainstream" religion, is likely to be transformed beyond present-day recognition in any case.

If these enthusiasms represent one extreme, then the fascination with Eastern, African, or primitive religion will continue to tantalize from the other. Transformation will more likely occur than translation. Borrowing of modes will be regular, but adoption and entrenchment of these styles will be more difficult. That is, Western religion looks and feels different once one has permitted Buddhism, Hinduism, and the like to refract a world, but it is not realistic to picture large numbers of people in the Christian churches making essential moves toward them.

The opening of wonder and the reinforcement of soul are both more likely to be profound and durable to the degree that their advocates revisit the Western meditative and mystical traditions. The yogi says to his European disciple after a long period of study, "No, you know about yoga, but you *are* not a yogi. You should not still be smoking the pipe. And your parents and forefathers should have been eating rice for a thousand years. Go back to your world, your books, your spiritual leaders."

In the years of radical action and secular theology, talk about spiritual depth would have been out of place. In fact, the avant-garde was projecting its disappearance from the serious world. Not long after, a sense of impoverishment was felt among those where soul had been neglected. A Presbyterian editor, noting that Billy Graham, a "soul" evangelizer, was telling a Congress on Evangelism to notice the world of social action, while Harvey Cox, a theorist of social action, was asking people to fantasize and celebrate a liturgy, asked: Would it not be a refreshing irony of the '70s were Graham to become known as the social thinker and Cox a pastor in care of souls?

Such a reversal is not likely to occur on a grand scale, but the school of thought that each represents has shown surprising openness to that over which the other's camp was the chief custodian.

Something of a mishmash approach is present in the new spiritual openness. At a retreat center run by Roman Catholic nuns, I attended an evening devotion prepared by those sisters. They showed the film *Le Sourire* (*The Smile*), which had to do with a Buddhist novice monk. Much of the film was slow-paced, silent or nearly so, and, shall we say, "Buddhist" in its senses of space and time. But the good sisters then filled in the void with passages from the Hebrew Scriptures, especially from the Psalms, on their own microphonic sound track. The language of "the Lord of hosts" was purposive, goal-directed, entirely out of keeping with the Buddhist visual material. One wonders whether either style is well served by such a mixing. It may be at best considered as early-stage eclecticism on the part of well-meaning people who are trying to absorb something new into their consciousness.

This openness to the East is accompanied by some measure of legitimate appropriation of "the soft revolution." Not all of Christian history has been as grim and productive as 1960s-style Protestantism and Catholicism were. Care of the small cell and of the person has often before implied a regard for bodies, for gestures and nuances. It is hard to rewrite Christian history and overlook its frequent ascetic tendencies; a second run at that history cannot make it look as if all led up to the plot of *The Sensuous Christian*. But the pietist "little churches inside the big church" and the early Methodist class meetings are only two examples of persistent appearances of encounter groups as locales for accepting and caring. The Christians who have re-

vived these today, with a little help from their friends at
Psychology Today, are operating with good warrant.

Sometimes, however, as a person observes the fumbling over
a restored "kiss of peace" or amateur stabs at sensitivity training,
he or she may wonder just how deep the Christian contribution
or commitment in these efforts can be. Is this another tag-along
movement, an adjustment of a weathervane? The more extravagant claims for Christian sensuousness and intensive encounter-
ing, the injunctions to forget one's mind and revel in the senses,
lead the historically informed observer to his own reverie. What
if this conversion occurred just before society at large began to
take another new turn, this time "back to reason"? There are
signs that people are seeing diminishing returns in the anti-
reason cults and are allowing for a chastened, qualified lauding
of reason to return. "The heart has its reasons that reason does
not know." Pascal was right. But the long Christian experience
with qualifying reason should prevent Christians from being
quickened to any glib faith in mad rationality. Therefore they
could become agents at restoring reason and civility.

FRESH ISSUES IN THE SEVENTIES

A ready acceptance of the challenge presented by a number
of issues or problems would be a fourth sign of life in today's
religion. No one can pretend that the public issues of the
decade past have been resolved or faced. There has even been
regress in the Nixonian era on racial justice, peacemaking, civil
liberties, the urban set of problems, and the like. But while
one can point to book-length bibliographies of religious ethical
writings on any of these matters, other areas have been under-
developed. A call for "benign neglect" on the grand themes
would be foolish, but new grand themes are coming to the fore.

For a sample: Any self-respecting minister or church librarian can point to rows of respectable books by blacks and whites on what to do about the racial problem. A potential reader who asks for even *one* good book on religion and the business ethic will be met by mutters and stutters. It is hard to name one volume by a competent and thoughtful theologian who has patiently dissected the ethos behind today's business and given clues for Christian action. Vice versa: the businessman who has shown that he has been informed by Christian theology as he set out with even a modestly inclusive approach to action in an apostolate to the business world evidently has written no books.

The odds in favor of acceptance of such a literature is high. The need is great. The churches, ministering as they so often do to the middle and upper-middle classes, are well poised to make an address. In the 1970s, after it became clear that a modified capitalism would survive and be reinforced, attention turned to the issues of humanizing that system. But while people on both sides of the conversation were inclined to say that it has broken down, accuracy should commit an observer to say that it has hardly begun.

The churches are positioned to contribute to solutions of the issues posed by aging. They are among the few voluntary agencies in society that have a multigenerational appeal. They could address "the last segregation," especially because their message commits them to. While the question about bombing in Southeast Asia was faced by elites that were far out of range of typical parishioners, the aged are a presence in all but the most age-stratified new suburbs or swingers' apartment areas in the city. The aged often live lonely, anxious, frightened lives. Health care among them is a scandal. They have great opportunities for being of help to each other and to others, to form communities of care. They have until recently tended to be overlooked except in institutional settings.

The extended family represents opportunities that forward-looking religionists are facing up to. Somewhere between the defensive or routine apologies for the cooped-up nuclear family and the free-form advocacy of wholly open families lies a field for future experiment. The ideal of Zero Population Growth will only reinforce the tendency that holds captive two children under roof with two or, as may be likely, one parent who survives the stress. The doors are shut. Grandparents do not live with their grandchildren in an age of one-story ranch homes and Social Security. Cousins are left behind in childhood.

Adoption, foster care, borrowing, and lending of children can all serve to open the family a bit. Arrangements of teamed families or collegial families of a quasi-communal character are available. They take the pressure off the too small and too tight family. They also, by the way, reflect more dimensions of the biblical concept of the family than do the modern accidental nuclear families in their splendid isolation. Churches have made tentative steps toward encouraging and appraising these ventures.

In combination with concern both for the aged and for the family is the possibility that the churches can contribute to interaction of the several generations. The very young and the very old have shown that they have interests in common over against the establishment generation. On other issues, the mid-career people found needed allies among both the older and the younger. But instead of encouraging these interactions, many churches supported stratifications based on age. Today they are beginning to desegregate on the basis of sex or age and allow for contacts that belie the validity of "generation gaps."

Ten years after the United States Supreme Court allowed

for the teaching about religion in elementary and secondary public schools, little had happened to help provide American children with intelligent approaches to the subject. Yet the hunger for teaching of values increased. Of course, religion and values come up in countless ways in the classrooms, but these are often informal and may well be haphazardly treated. On some aspects of values education, such as the topic of sex, religious groups have more often than not come on the scene as powers that were bent on staking out their own territories or projecting their own prejudices. But churches are also in the values game, and some of them have started to be reinforcing and encouraging groups, particularly in the states where textbooks on religion in education are beginning to appear. Enlivened communication channels between schools and churches are developing.

Medical ethics: Before the century is over, many experts predict that genetic tampering will have progressed through cloning to the point that the human race can choose what kind of people it would like to produce. The child will be the twin of the parent. The theoretical possibility has begun to exist, and many predict that not all laboratories or governments will permanently hold back from the experiment. The implications for a changed human nature are vast, dwarfing all other ethical issues and challenging even the population and thermonuclear questions. These matters will be voted upon and decided, accepted or rejected, by a populace that includes Christians who have much at stake. The theological community now numbers four or five recognized experts. That is all.

Questions of organ transplant, abortion, and euthanasia come up with increasing frequency. They are not decided in isolation far from local gatherings of Christians. They have to be faced daily in thousands of hospitals. Not a few of the physicians and nurses are members of or are willing to serve congregations and other religious units. Here is another outlet for energies.

Dr. Granger Westberg has developed an attractive program of medical care in the context of religion at Springfield, Ohio, and elsewhere. Free clinics are staged on church premises, with doctors and ministers or other religious counselors present. The doctors who donate their time on their day off say that the projects actually save them time in the long run. Many of the people soon announce a preference for religious counsel, since many of their problems are more of a spiritual than of a medical character. Westberg thinks such an alliance can be effected in many communities. Another field of service will thereby open. It will make explicit use of the Christian energies and viewpoints of people.

Law: The "Good Samaritan" laws are only one of many issues that have to be faced in growing inquiries between lawyers and their lay counterparts and clienteles in religious circles. Now that the drug problem is universal, as at home in the suburbs as in the ghettos, the churches are making efforts to understand and serve where once ignorance ruled. The problem of crime is a moral problem in which the churches have a vital stake; attitudes toward penal reform, the death penalty, and law and order are usually rooted in doctrines of man and society. Almost no congregation is out of range of addressing the issues, but not many have yet taken them up. Investment policies of local units are as ethically complicated as are those of national organizations. Shall church funds be invested in institutions that can help minorities, or, at least, be withheld from those that hurt them?

The matter of amnesty for draft exiles in Canada would be a good test case of Christians' commitments to familial life and reconciliation or of their sense of either vengeance or calculation about the draft in future wars. There are no easy answers on either side. The President added great emotional heat to the issue in an election campaign. In a cooler moment or at some distance from exploitative power in Washington, a fresh comment based on new attitudes could be prepared and eventual change effected. Some churches are beginning to take part.

These are homely and sometimes domestic illustrations. They are significant because while local churches can have something to do with them, they are all locked into national and international problems that have only begun to be faced. Not all the expertise that is necessary can be developed locally. Some of the grass-roots mystique will be dispelled as people learn the need for theological schools, law and medical schools, and the like. And elites in those schools will find that a new realism enters their inquiries as a result of such contacts. "We are members one of another."

NEW RECRUITS

This rather cheerful and programmatic chapter, which has erupted in the midst of our culture's all-pervading gloom, has to include as another asset or direction the fact that new recruits are on the scene and new alliances are possible. If Jesus people find out what "doing the will of Jesus' father" may mean in their own discipleship, many of them will have to turn to more complex expressions than their first burst of faith permitted them. If Pentecostals grow a bit weary of their original Spirit experience or find it hard to transmit to the young or to apply to all circumstances, they can bring new life to the whole religious scene if they recognize that "there are a variety of gifts, but the same spirit."

As a result of the evangelism efforts, there could be a transfusion of new talent across the spectrum of the churches. While the success-minded churches are best tooled to pile on more successes, not all the new converts and recruits can be permanently at home in the churches that possess special competences for tracking them down. If the past is any precedent, the resources of the church catholic will be needed. They provide many options for people who change from what they were when the revivalist or doorbell ringer first reached them. Many of the more conventional churches' periodical literature has reflected the need for their members to understand the care and feeding of freaks and Pentecostalists who come into their orbit.

Little more need be added about the growing variety of witnesses in the fast-growing churches. The evangelicals are having to make room for an impressive group of social critics who are dispelling pictures of monolithic support for the status quo on the part of evangelicals. Richard V. Pierard had called the linking of evangelical Christianity and political conservatism *The Unequal Yoke*. He opens his chapters with quotations he and his colleagues resent.

"There's good reason to mix religion and politics. . . . We have found that fundamentalist Christians and conservative politicians have a lot in common." Thus said the chaplain of the Georgia Senate. A Christian Crusader: "For any self-respecting person, any person who loves his country and fears God, there is no such thing as the middle of the road. A special place in hell is being reserved for people who believe in walking down the middle of the political and religious road. It will be their privilege to fry. . . ." A respected evangelical minister: "Firmness is the only thing which Communists understand. Firmness must be backed up by military strength and force." A Reformed theologian: "Only a return to orthodox Christianity can shatter the messianic humanism of the United Nations."

Pierard counters this anthology of naïve-to-evil proclamations with counter testimony showing that conservative evangelicalism can and should relate to a number of political options. Perhaps the last thing America needs is a simple identification of evangelicalism now, in its turn, with a liberal political program. But it is showing a richer sense of choice, more freedom. If the more static churches experience declining power, it is important to see new energies come up among the fast-growing ones. Pierard can cite former Congressman John B. Anderson, Lester De Koster, Senator Mark O. Hatfield, Carl F. H. Henry, T. B. Maston, David O. Moberg, John H. Redekop, and Foy Valentine as other authors across this part of the spectrum. It is not necessarily valid or useful for social actionists who are not of the evangelical camp to overadvertise their presence or exaggerate their contribution—it would only make life more difficult for them. But a few quiet hurrahs are in order.

THE NEED FOR INTERPRETERS

In a gray season this canvass of new peoples, vital local units, personal and spiritual concern, new outlets for service, and new potential alliances suggests the need for a community of interpretation. Because of their inability to come up immediately with new paradigms or models, intellectuals in Christianity were often discredited. When the culture as a whole downgraded learning, as a glance at its priorities in the early 1970s shows it to be doing, it is difficult for them to regain their place in the catholic scheme of things. When the excitements are off somewhere with ecstatic or sensuous Christianity, it is often a bit lonely for the people who quietly remind church members that they will also have to think. But the academy has survived, humbled and more diffident than in the past, but still adventurous.

The college classrooms of the 1970s replaced the chapel of the 1960s as a campus locale for determining how religion relates to meaning and values. The occult interest in the late 1960s and the Jesus phenomena of the early 1970s reopened the doors of some sanctuaries. But many students let their peers and their teachers know that they have to make sense of the world of Jew and Gentile, Protestant and Catholic, Buddhist-Hindu and Westerner, believer and atheist. They have to piece together meaning where a tradition was not well transmitted to them. They have to overcome crises of identity. They care about cloning and amnesty, about abortion and aging, about truth claims and the validity of experiences.

For these reasons it is hard to picture that the whole religious future belongs to the enthusiasts or the go-getters. The latter can address some aspects of faith and life, but fall short in decisive areas. Peter Berger has predicted that with increasing secularization, by the end of the century, surviving Christianity would represent "cognitive minorities." That means that they would be made up of people who look and see and think about different things in different ways than do the worldlings around them. George Lindbeck, noting these trends, had prophesied a "sectarian future" for the churches. They would not be linked; they would be cut off from the disciplines and the powers.

In the rhythms of Christian response, some retreat to sects and cognitive minorities is necessary for people to gain a point of view from which to interpret the reality around the church. But after retreat comes an advance, in Jewish terms, to the hallowing of all of life, or to "all things" which cohere in Christ, to follow a Christian way of speaking. Without these connections, religion is incomplete and, in the long pull of things, uncreative if not actually threatening.

A colleague once told me how he would find support for

the community of interpretation wherein religion has its place wherever learning goes on. "Sell it like you sold sex education ten years ago. It's dangerous to be ignorant. There is going to be a lot of religion around, and an awful lot of it is harmful to humans unless interpreted. Society had better become alert to this. Of course, that's only the beginning; there is a whole ladder of positives, too."

A community of interpretation will have greater difficulty carrying out its mandates if the ecstatic spiritualism or success-minded organizationalism in religion long prevail. Unless these are challenged or complemented, there will be a new void in the lives of a generation. Life is not only interpretation and thought, and the energy provided by the aggressive religious movements at the turn of the decade can contribute to wholeness. The uninterpreted life is not worth living, and the over-interpreted life is not living. But the new breach between Athens and Jerusalem, between the academy and the community of faith, between mind and heart ill serves religious or social forces or the persons who make up both. "Because we are present to a world," says Merleau-Ponty, "we are condemned to meaning." Not all meaning comes from the momentary experience of coming to Jesus or signing up on a church roll, even if in the excitement of a moment the promise seems rich. If those who have taken on the burden of interpretation in the past now abdicate, their place will have to be taken up by new clusters and lineages.

8

Coring

Where there has been "the closing off of identity, the constriction of self-process, . . . straight-and-narrow specialization in psychological as well as in intellectual life, and . . . reluctance to let in any extraneous influence," religious movements have been growing. Where they have been open, expansive, Protean, and ready to absorb outside influences, they have more often than not been static or declining. The first style takes a toll in wholeness, fullness, and catholicity. The second is high-risk, and fails when it lacks a center.

The mainline religious forces in America are not in position to erect high boundaries. They seek some discipline and definition, but they would deny their fundamental grasp of what it is to be "in Christ" if they used that experience to build impassable walls. But that characteristic need not prevent them from reorienting themselves to the task of finding their center. To the degree that they succeed, they can regain a responsible place in the religious field and take on missions the intransigents are unable and unwilling to assume.

For this task of centering, we can entertain a term that has been appropriate both in anatomy or psychology and in the foundry. The endeavor involves a search for the core of Christian experience and tradition. The core is *"the central or uni-*

versal part, the 'heart'" of anything. And to core is *"to mold or cast with a core."*

A university president discussing persons who had been recommended to him for a vice-presidency kept asking: "Has this person a core?" What did he mean? "Oh, anyone can glibly relate to other persons and things around him; has he a heart or a center so that others have to relate to him?" That center or universal part, that heart cannot be "cut out" and left over, or easily located and defined. So in the realm of religion, however many shapes the outer part of its mold may assume, there has to be casting with a core.

The constrictive model in religion builds walls of orthodoxy or orthopraxis less out of love of truth, says Eric Hoffer, than from a sense of mutual suspicion among the adherents. The expansive version of religious styles simply sprawls and blurs. But a "cored" alternative has a magnetic center, which allows for openness at the edges.

To speak of a core in Christianity is not to be able to point to an essence of the faith. We were all through that effort decades ago, in the days of German scholar Adolf von Harnack, when people wanted to define a kernel or an essence. "The fatherhood of God and the brotherhood of man" served for some. But coring as we use it is a process and not an achievement, an intention and not a fulfillment. To claim achievements and fulfillments would result in the constrictive, high-walled solution and cut off catholic possibility.

Coring is the opposite tendency from that chosen in the open churches in the recent past. The bureaucrats in complex organizations did not build around a core, because they were specialized and dealt with their part, their territory. The "generals without armies" were interested in the uses of power without devoting themselves to the spiritual center of Christian life. The revolutionaries did not care about the problem at all. The worldly or secular theologians wanted to phase off into the world. Most of them asked how far they could be from the act of coring and still be considered Christian, for some reasons good or bad. The survival of effective catholic Christianity depends upon the ability of significant confessors and professors to reverse this tendency, and this reversal has begun. The end of the cult of relevance or at least the signs of its impending demise could be taken as promising signals that people will be free to engage in coring, in seeking the universal or the heart.

PROGRAMMING AND TRADITION

Why? First of all, because, to use a term that Hans Küng and I saw emerge between us one summer day, the Christian community is "genetically programmed" around a nucleus of a core that is the experience of the love of God in Jesus Christ. This programming is read out of the charter documents of the Christian scripture. While it need not be constrictive—even its canon is open—it is centered, or cored. To speak of wanting to be a Christian without some reference to the central *traditum*, the "tradition" of what God handed over in Christ, leads only to confusion. Another name should be sought by people who would avoid the reference.

This *traditum* is handed down through a Christian lore that cannot be neat or bordered. It has been Eastern and Western, Catholic and Orthodox and Protestant, made up of countless emphases and forces through many centuries in many places. But the key turns it took are available to the community through the records. Beyond the Bible and the historical record, the Christian continues coring activities through a regard for the surrounding culture, since that culture always is bonded to the expressions of the faith. Finally, constructive reason can be brought to bear not to provide faith or to prove the existence of God but to relate that culture or world to the grasp of faith in scripture and tradition.

The simplest Christians may engage in such coring more effectively than do specialists. They have a way of comprehending something of what the "universal or heart" of the matter has been and is. But cores are not out of range of those who deal willingly with complexity. When successful, or to the degree that it is successful, the coring church can prevent itself from simply following every fad or fancy.

A NEW WAY OF SEEING

Coring does not mean being content with golden means or middling affairs; it has nothing to do with humdrum and bourgeois faith and life. While traditions can wear at the edges of something that had once been, there is nothing average or settled about the concerns of the Christian faith. Reference to it does not therefore mean that we have wearied of attempts to present alternatives to the world as it is and are settling for ballast, for settling back in a kind of neoconservative adaptation. "If any one is in Christ, there is a new world." Such a biblical text is affirmed by evangelical and "liberal" churches alike; it ought to represent a vast distancing from those who do not see the world the same way. Much depends upon the way of seeing.

Carlos Castaneda's *A Separate Reality* includes a metaphor about seeing, though in a different context:

> "Once you learn, you can *see* every single thing in the world in a different way."
> "Then, Don Juan, you don't see the world in the usual way any more."
> "I see both ways. When I want to *look* at the world I

see it the way you do. Then when I want to *see* it, I look
at it the way I know and I perceive it in a different way."

"But . . . what's the advantage of learning to see?"

"You can tell things apart. You can see them for what
they really are."

The Christian does not look out on a different world, but "in
Christ" he sees things for what they really are. To be "in
Christ" in catholic Christianity does not mean that one has
come to him in only one way. The Jesus people's refinement of
the process is canceled out in the light of the New Testament's
164 uses of the formula "in Christ" and its cognates. They provide nothing so much as a kind of all-pervasive envelope or situation. To be in Christ is to share his situations, his circumstances.

What matters is the new world which the person "in Christ"
sees. The field of vision or horizon changes. The old order has
already gone; the new order is already here. This perspective or
new vision encompasses everything. It is at the root of the catholic concept of Christianity, a faith that has a center but is less
concerned with borders. Father Walter Ong reminds us that behind the term "Catholic" lie both a Latin concept and a Greek.
The Greek concept is the more positive one; *katholikos* means
literally "through-the-whole." "The concept has a positive, out-
going quality to it. Instead of pulling things in around a center,
it moves out to all things. In the concept of catholic, 'through-
the-whole,' there is no hint of fencing in. Rather, what is catholic floods being with itself. Let being grow, expand, as much as
you will, what is Catholic will grow and expand with it, filling
its every nook and cranny."

DEVELOPMENTAL CATHOLICITY

Thus catholicity has an "expansive, positive quality as against
the pinched, impoverished, forced, and quite unpersuasive 'uni-

versal.' . . . The universalist . . . wishes to pull things in to himself. The Catholic wants to give himself to others, to go out to them in an expansive movement of love, even more than E. E. Cummings' father, who 'moved through dooms of love . . . singing each new leaf out of each tree.' "

It seems hardly necessary to point out that such a concept of cored, "catholic" Christianity does not belong to Orthodox or Roman Catholic Christianity alone. Protestantism can share it. It is hard to build a club or a sect around the concept. Indeed, the idea of a sect on one hand and a faith marked by the desire to be *katholikos* on the other are mutually contradictory. I learned in 1968 how difficult it is to be partisan about developmental catholic views. The Reverend Robert Campbell, O.P., in *Spectrum of Protestant Beliefs,* interviewed five Protestants and placed them on the spectrum, including "Fundamentalism," "Evangelicalism," "Confessionalism," "Liberalism," and "Radicalism." He asked the five spokesmen to estimate how many followers each had. Then he did his own estimating and decided that there were 23.5 million fundamentalists, 15.5 million new evangelicals, 8.0 million confessionalists, 20.5 million liberals, and 0.1 million radicals. His chosen radical, however, was more modest. William Hamilton wrote, ". . . the people that are professionally committed to the radical theology in both what I call the conservative form that I represent and the somewhat more radical form . . . must be considered quite small—100 to 200 men and women."

Where did "catholic" Protestantism fit on this sequence of bands? The introduction included a sentence that gave them a comeuppance: "It might also be asked why there was no inclusion of what might be called 'developmental theology'—Martin E. Marty, Robert McAfee Brown, Jaroslav Pelikan, etc. It was felt that these . . . writers represent an articulate segment of publishing theologians but their views are not typical of a large identifiable segment of popular Protestant beliefs and attitudes." This means that if Hamilton's radicals could be included with as few as a hundred adherents, the "developmental" approach—assuming that the word is appropriate—if it had at least three spokesmen, could hope to number at most ninety-seven followers. A scraggly band, hardly identifiable.

Enough statistical fun and games. This approach did not even show up on Campbell's spectrum as a "large identifiable segment," because it is not a segment so much as a way of seeing, not an end product but a process, not a Protestant club in the first place but a pan-Christian emphasis. While it is born of a vision of Christ in all his simplicity, it would reach "through-the-whole," and thus can be enjoyed only by those who tolerate and even relish complexity, "the whole counsel of God."

"People often stumble over the truth," says Winston Churchill, "but they pick themselves up and hurry along as if nothing had happened." A truth over which Christians repeatedly stumble is the one that asserts that Jesus Christ has to do with "all things." They pick themselves up and keep restricting him, fencing themselves in, and ruling out the various disciplines and areas of life or vocations as being beyond their scope. They do all this constricting so as not to see the dissolution of their identities. But if a life or a philosophy has a core, or heart, risks can be taken.

THE PATH OF MEDITATION

How does centering, or coring, occur as a step toward the expansive catholic vision? Among the ways are meditation, interpretation, and creation.

Meditation. Christianity conscious of coring will not abandon itself to being only productive. But instead of having to pretend that it can deal from within with the world's many centers (Eastern, African, occult), it takes the route the Jesus people and the Pentecostalists do, by concentrating on the historical experience that vivifies Christianity. The late Thomas Merton is typical of those who took the path of contemplation. "Whatever I may have written, I think it all can be reduced in the end to this one root truth: that God calls human persons to union with himself and with one another in Christ."

The call of God produces a change in the human community. Eugen Rosenstock-Huessy would replace Descartes's rationalist model (*Cogito ergo sum,* I think, therefore I am) with a responsive one, *Respondeo etsi mutabor,* I respond although I will be changed. This responding offers an altered consciousness, a foretaste of a future way of looking at reality, a new perspective. It belongs to both the community and the individual. The meditative way shares the quest for the immediate experience with the enthusiasts and the ecstatics. It recognizes that people are contingent beings, born for a life of relationship.

The goal of the religiously altered consciousness has little in common with the drug-induced experience, hypnosis, trance, and the like. It involves a "centering," which begins by a purging from the responding being of all extraneous elements, a voiding so that one can focus on "God calling human persons to union with himself and with one another in Christ." This practice sets out to transcend ordinary, workaday, everyday experience. The ordinary is what produces wars and pollution and the humdrum. The extraordinary way disengages people from the frantic pursuit of gain and the attempts to exploit others.

The path of meditation is regarded as having intrinsic validity; it does not have to be productive of secondary benefits any more than does the playing of a Beethoven string quartet. The benefits belong to what might be inferred from Christ's remembered word about the promise of a more abundant life. But there are side boons, including empathy with the non-Western world, which lives more easily with nature and silence and a way of defining the person apart from "necessity," from what he or she produces. For these and other reasons, those concerned both with power and with the care of souls are taking more care of the interior life and are learning or teaching again the arts of meditating, centering, or following the devotional path.

THE WAYS OF THE INTERPRETER

The immediate experience is not necessarily easily, readily, or constantly available. More of the time, people must spend time interpreting their experience. This is the occasion for theology. That theology has come upon bad times hardly needs saying. The giant shapers of thought are gone. An intermediate generation has failed to find a convincing voice. Some current spokesmen are often so specialized and technical that they lack impact on the people of God or the larger society. But something that has been historically represented by the term theology continues to go on. It may be in the hands of autobiographers, narrators, historians, or novelists and poets. They may be finding a new paradigm or model by stumbling upon a very old one.

Whatever may be true elsewhere, American thought about religion cannot longer be contained in the Greek-German forms that came to provide almost exhaustive definitions in much of the theological world for some decades. In some moments the abstract and idealist-existentialist approach has spoken with power. It may come back and speak to minorities with freshness in the future. But, from the beginning, theologians have puzzled over why people on these shores do not pay more at-

tention to that Germanic theology which follows Greek outlines. Jonathan Edwards sensed that his work needed a new
cast. He resolved to do theology in a new mold, the historical
one. His first experiments were inelegant, but the astute revivalist had pierced the heart or core of his people with that
observation. His interpretations of colonial life were later to be
reshaped and become very widespread in Protestantism.

Abraham Lincoln is sometimes seen as a theologian of the
American experience because of the way he interpreted the life
of a people. Walter Rauschenbusch, the social-gospel leader,
was effective because he took core biblical and historical themes
and used them to point directions for the turn-of-the-century
American people. Reinhold Niebuhr wondered at times whether
he should be considered a theologian at all: he was a preacher,
prophet, politician, journalist, spinning out his view in countless editorial comments on a passing scene. Father John Court-
ney Murray devoted his best self to reflecting on the meaning
of the American people's distinctive experiences in the political
order.

In each case they worked, in part, with an older and, one is
tempted to say, Hebraic model. They dealt concretely with the
happenings of a people. Theology in this definition is the interpretation of the life of a people in the light of a transcendent
reference. God does not have to be accounted for in each minute detail and with utter confidence. Lincoln said that the Al-
mighty had his own purposes; Niebuhr said that the Psalmist
was right: "He that sitteth in the heavens shall laugh" when
prideful nations overidentify with Him. Edwards cannot be
accused of deserting either the concept of divine mystery or the
integrity of the ideal world. But one side of their activity had
special power, because they operated out of a core vision and

then let it apply to the many dimensions of life, let it move "through-the-whole," not fenced in or constricted.

Such a concept is full of hazards. The autobiographical mode can become narcissistic or boring if the writer has not had profound experiences to interpret. The dangers of overidentification with one people (e.g. The Americans, The Baptists, The Blacks, The Liberals) are present, but the men just cited were not guilty of losing the prophets' note, which says that God judges one's own group. Being ready to confine God to one's interpretations of detail on the one hand, or to see him as so remote from the whole process that all meaning is lost, are additional concerns. To speak of a public theology or one focused on peoplehood is not to solve theological problems but only to locate a milieu for one way of interpreting reality that is somehow congruent with modern Westerners' ways of looking at the world: empirically, historically, practically, and the like.

If the academic community lacks interest in such reflection, the public will turn elsewhere for sustenance. The popularity of apocalypticists like Hal Lindsey or radio evangelists like the Armstrongs, resides in their eagerness to identify every detail of biblical prophecy with events in the day's newspapers. Core Christianity cannot indulge in such quests for popularity through sensation, but it can learn how and why certain approaches to theology can minister to a public. In the Jewish world the late rabbi Abraham Joshua Heschel kept alive the dialectic of transcendence and involvement, responsiveness to ancient scripture and alertness to contemporary happenings—without letting either pole dissolve into the other.

THE TASKS OF CREATION

The third way of seeing core Christianity emerge in process is through creation. Creation has two dimensions: *poiesis* and *praxis.* Poiesis, the word behind "poetry," is creation as the gods create. Jakob Boehme, the Protestant mystic, spoke of "the *drive, life, spirit, elasticity,* or *torment* of matter" as he pointed to the raw material behind creation. "Poiesis," says Jacques Lefebvre, "gives human form to the sensuous; it includes man's relations with nature . . . the appropriation of nature by human beings, both of the nature external to themselves and that which is internal to themselves."

Poiesis lies behind the sense of wonder that environmentalists say has to be stimulated again and behind the celebration of Christian mysteries to which the liturgists call their fellow believers. It is, in one scholar's terms, "pointless but significant." It is not full of point in the productive sense, but it signs the transcendent. Goethe: "I have never bothered or asked in what way I was useful to society as a whole; I contented myself with expressing what I recognized as good and true. That has certainly been useful in a wide circle; but that was not the aim; it was the necessary result."

With this is linked praxis, "a universal-creative self-creative activity, activity by which man transforms and creates his world and himself." "Man can never be completely finished," continues Gajo Petrovic; "he is not man when he lives only in the present and in the contemplation of the past, but only in so far as he in the present realizes his future. Man is man if he realizes his historically created human possibilities."

In this sense, "coring" involves using the central motifs of Christianity to create a new environment in which the good can occur. Here is the passing on of the glass of cold water, the housing of the beggar, the building of a better society, the doing what any situation demands. The American Christian avant-garde in the early 1960s can be accused of having isolated and having been obsessed by the theme of *praxis,* while his successor at the end of the decade in the religious analogues to the "counter culture" was preoccupied with *poiesis*. He began to lose a sense of responsibility for the environment. We picture "coring" going on when the two are creatively interplayed.

If it has been necessary for just a moment to sound technical, this is not because the activities implied cannot be carried on by any but the elite. The "soul" singer, rich in *poiesis*, did not need to be highly literate. She also knew something about *praxis*. Thus Mahalia Jackson: "I'm going to live the life I sing about in my song." Because this dual vision has to deal with complexity, it must allow for elites. Theological work is hard, creation of works of art demands expertise, interpreting a world demands competences. But elit*ism* is not the intended or permissible effect. "Core" Christianity is available to all people and develops in patterns congruent with their perceptions of a world.

HUMANISM AND PROPHECY

This catholic picture calls for a strange blend of Christian humanism and prophecy. The absence of humanism leads to selfish and destructive life, since no responsibility is taken for culture. The absence of prophecy produces static life and contributes only to ballast and security. Can the two be combined? Can one have Erasmus with Christian humanism and Jacques Ellul with the prophetic note at the same time? Can one be devoted to learning and culture on one hand and call learning and culture into question on the other? The Jewish example of Abraham Joshua Heschel and the Christian instance of Thomas Merton suggest that some models have begun to emerge in the twentieth century. They are both known for their humanism and for the effectiveness of their judgment upon an unjust society.

Ellul, whose analysis of technology and whose Barthian theology we need not entirely enjoy, did distance Christians from their own movements and clubs, and kept the transcendent note alive. The Christian "is a man of the future, not of a temporal and logical future, but of the *eschaton*, of the coming break with this present world." Not to play with worldly concepts of revolution but to be really radical and revolutionary in the Christian sense—and this upsets all who provide societal ballast—"is to judge the world by its present state, by actual facts, in the name of a truth which does not yet exist (but is coming)—and it is to do so, because we believe this truth to be more genuine and more real than the reality which surrounds us." "It is not [the Christian's] primary task to think out plans, programmes, methods of action and of achievement. When Christians do this (and there is an epidemic of this behaviour at the present time in the Church) it is simply an imitation of the world, which is doomed to defeat. What *we* can do is of no importance unless we can offer it with a 'good conscience toward God.'"

"A man who spends all his time in action, by that very fact ceases to live. . . . What matters is to *live,* and not to act. In this world, this is a revolutionary attitude, for the world only desires [utilitarian] action, and has no desire for *life* at all." But over against this prophetic note there is also the Christian's loving concern for the world, his care for the earth, the person, the community. That is the point of origin and the point itself of a Christian humanism for tomorrow.

CARING AND CORING

For some years I have been pondering a text by Hannah Arendt, one that worked its way into a chapter title, belongs in a book title, and has been the theme behind this essay against constriction in an age of constrictive tendencies, and against dissolution and shipwreck in a threatening time. She refers to traditional political authority, but her word can be applied to other kinds of authority as well:

"Authority, resting on a foundation in the past as its unshaken cornerstone, gave the world the permanence and durability which human beings need precisely because they are mortals—the most unstable and futile beings we know of. Its loss is tantamount to the loss of the groundwork of the world, which indeed since then has begun to shift, to change and transform itself with ever-increasing rapidity from one shape into another, as though we were living and struggling with a Protean universe where everything at any moment can become almost anything else."

She concludes her section with a motif that cannot be permitted to stand for *less* than Christian humanism intends: "But the loss of worldly permanence and reliability—which politically is identical with the loss of authority—does not entail, at least not necessarily, the loss of the human capacity for building, preserving, and caring for a world that can survive us and remain a place fit to live in for those who come after us." Such caring, for a Christian, is still another way to "light the fire" of a sacred place.

Caring and coring belong together in the Christian world. When brought together, they offer the beginning of possibility for new vision, new consciousness, a new world, the spark of a new fire that we can light in a dark age.

REFERENCE NOTES

The design of this book, which is a sort of personal essay, did not call for extensive footnoting, and not every reference—particularly to aphorisms or phrases—is documented. But some readers may wish to see the larger context in which some of the cited materials first appeared. For that reason I append a number of book titles and journal articles referred to in passing in the text.

The opening story, from which the book's title is drawn, is taken from Gershom G. Scholem, *Major Trends in Jewish Mysticism* (New York: Schocken, 1961), pp. 349f.

FOREWORD
Several times these passages will be cited from Robert Jay Lifton, *Boundaries: Psychological Man in Revolution* (New York: Vintage, 1970), pp. 37f., 43f., and 51.

1. ALWAYS KEEP A HOLD ON NURSE

THE FORMAL SYSTEM
On this concept see Charles Hampden-Turner, *Radical Man: The Process of Psycho-Social Development* (Cambridge, Mass.: Schenkman, 1970), Chapter VI, pp. 127ff.; the Belloc lines are on p. 151.

FREEDOM AND EQUALITY SEEM SECONDARY
Carl L. Becker's essay appears in *Detachment and the Writing of History: Essays and Letters of Carl L. Becker* (Ithaca, N.Y.: Cornell, 1958), pp. 188ff.

ELITE DEFENSE OF THE CONSENSUS

Lowell D. Streiker and Gerald S. Strober, *Religion and the New Majority: Billy Graham, Middle America, and the Politics of the 70s* (New York: Association Press, 1972), pp. 189f.

THE MYSTICAL MILLENNIUM

The book titles alluded to in the first paragraph of this section are Charles A. Reich, *The Greening of America* (New York: Random House, 1970), William Braden, *The Private Sea* (Chicago: Quadrangle, 1967), and Theodore Roszak, *The Making of a Counter Culture* (Garden City, N.Y.: Doubleday, 1969). Senghor is quoted in John V. Taylor, *The Primal Vision* (Philadelphia: Fortress, 1963), p. 21. Margaret Mead's theory of generations appears in her *Culture and Commitment: A Study of the Generation Gap* (Garden City, N.Y.: Natural History Press, 1970).

NEW CONSCIOUSNESS

See John Cooper, *The New Mentality* (Philadelphia: Westminster, 1969), pp. 9ff. for an enthusiastic announcement of the new sensibility and human type.

WHEN CRISIS COMES

Ortega is quoted in Karl J. Weintraub, *Visions of Culture* (Chicago: University of Chicago, 1966), p. 281. For *anomie*, refer again to Hampden-Turner, op. cit., pp. 140ff. The second Ortega quotation appears in Weintraub, op. cit., p. 269. The final Hampden-Turner reference is to *Radical Man*, pp. 68f.

2. THAT'S NICE, DON'T FIGHT

SPIRITUALITY SUPPRESSED

While the symposium on Religion in America subsequently appeared in two paperback books, the original papers were gathered in *Daedalus*, Winter 1967. Most of the quotations derive from my chapter, pp. 99ff.

SUPERNATURALISM AND SOUL

On secularity and new religiousness, Herman Kahn and Anthony J. Wiener, *The Year 2000* (New York: Macmillan, 1967), pp. 39 and 48. See also Robert Boguslaw, *The New Utopians: A Study of*

System Design and Social Change (Englewood Cliffs, N.J.: Prentice-Hall, 1965).

THE AMERICAN EXCEPTION

The changes wrought by industrial and urban society are discussed in Thomas Luckmann, *The Invisible Religion* (New York: Macmillan, 1967), especially in Chapter II, "Church-Oriented Religion on the Periphery of Modern Society."

THE ACCENT ON EXPERIENCE

Herman Kahn, op. cit., p. 48.

THE NEW MOVEMENTS

For a fuller discussion of the persistence of rite and myth, Andrew M. Greeley, *Unsecular Man: The Persistence of Religion* (New York: Schocken, 1972) is helpful. Other recent books that discuss the new movements are Jacob Needleman, *The New Religions* (Garden City, N.Y.: Doubleday, 1970), and Peter Rowley, *New Gods in America* (New York: David McKay, 1971).

3. OPEN AND SHUT CASES

PROTEAN MAN

Treating nature "as if" it is magical is advocated in Roszak, op. cit., p. 244; see also Harvey Cox, *Feast of Fools* (Cambridge: Harvard University Press, 1969).

CONSTRICTION: SHUT CASES

The Fitzgerald quotation appears in Hampden-Turner, op. cit., p. 37. The Lifton references are in *Boundaries* (see note under "Foreword").

TWO DENOMINATIONAL FATES

The map to which this whole section refers is inserted in Edwin Scott Gaustad, *Historical Atlas of Religion in America* (New York: Harper, 1962).

WHO GROWS WHEN?

Dean M. Kelley, *Why Conservative Churches Are Growing* (New

York: Harper & Row, 1972) is an important resource for the argument in this whole chapter, and should be consulted.

4. CLAY FEET CLEAR UP TO OUR NAVEL

FASCINATIONS WITH SUCCESS

For the sources of the McCabe incident, see my *The Infidel: Freethought and American Religion* (Cleveland: World, 1961), pp. 161ff.

INVISIBLE GROWTH AND REVOLVING DOORS

Henry P. Van Dusen's article appeared in *Life,* June 9, 1958, pp. 122–24.

THE NEW MARKS OF THE CHURCH

What are here called "new marks" are detailed by Kelley, op. cit., pp. 58ff. On the sixth mark, fanaticism, see Josef Rudin, *Fanaticism* (Notre Dame, Ind.: University of Notre Dame, 1969), especially p. 37.

THE SIMPLE AND THE COMPLEX

On Methodism and Pietism, Alfred North Whitehead, *Adventures of Ideas* (New York: Mentor edition, 1955), pp. 30f.

THE WORLDLINESS OF THE OTHERWORLDLY

The Texan Baptist millionaire makes his appearance in David Martin, *The Religious and the Secular* (New York: Schocken, 1969), pp. 11f.

5. WITHOUT BOUNDARIES OR CENTER

OPEN AND CENTERED

Robert Jay Lifton, op. cit., pp. 43ff., one more time.

6. NEARSIGHTED LEADERS, BLIND-SIDERS, AND RECOVERY

ORGANIZATIONALISM

Henry J. Pratt, *The Liberalization of American Protestantism: A Case Study in Complex Organizations* (Detroit: Wayne State University Press, 1972). See also the work of Etzioni on which Pratt is most dependent, Amitai Etzioni, *Modern Organizations* (Englewood Cliffs, N.J.: Prentice-Hall, 1964).

My own essay on COCU in its crisis appeared in Paul Crow, Jr., and William Jerry Boney, *Church Union at Midpoint* (New York: Association, 1972), pp. 178ff.

BLIND-SIDED FROM THE LEFT

For the program of the liberal, see Pratt, op. cit., p. 13. Clergy-lay tensions are described in Jeffrey K. Hadden, *The Gathering Storm in the Churches: The Widening Gap between Clergy and Laymen* (Garden City, N.Y.: Doubleday, 1969). On supporting the "interesting" poor, if it advances one's own cause, see Jacques Ellul, *Violence: Reflections from a Christian Perspective* (New York: Seabury, 1969), pp. 67ff. The *Theology Today* article referred to is Robert Banks, "How Revolutionary Is Revolutionary Theology?" (January 1972; XXVII, 4), pp. 394ff.

The apologia for politics that has impressed me most recently is Bernard Crick, *In Defence of Politics* (Harmondsworth, Middlesex: Penguin, 1964); see especially pp. 141ff.

SECULAR THEOLOGY AND BOUNDARYLESSNESS

Two attacks on the myth of secular man are the books by Andrew Greeley and David Martin, both referred to above.

On the breakup of paradigms, Thomas S. Kuhn, *The Structure of Scientific Revolutions* (Chicago: University of Chicago Press, 1962). For a number of suggestions that the world of mystic distance was being dispelled, see Thomas J. J. Altizer and William Hamilton, *Radical Theology and the Death of God* (Indianapolis: Bobbs-Merrill, 1966); Hamilton's illustrations are particularly pithy and to the point.

Monika Hellwig's book review appeared in *Cross Currents*, Spring 1972 (XXII, 2), pp. 210ff.

SPIRITUAL EXPRESSION AND PERSONALISM

Dietrich von Oppen, *The Age of the Person: Society in the Twentieth Century* (Philadelphia: Fortress, 1969). See Sam Keen, *To a Dancing God* (New York: Harper & Row, 1970) and Thomas F. Oden, *The Intensive Group Experience: The New Pietism*

(Philadelphia: Westminster, 1972), for personal and small-group evaluations from differing theological points of view.

7. WE ARE CONDEMNED TO MEANING

HELP FROM THE SHIPWRECKED

Ortega is quoted by Weintraub, op. cit., p. 286.

NEW RECRUITS

Richard V. Pierard, *The Unequal Yoke: Evangelical Christianity and Political Conservatism* (New York: Lippincott, 1970), is a representative and helpful comment on evangelicalism's political dilemmas.

THE NEED FOR INTERPRETERS

Merleau-Ponty is quoted in Huston Smith, *Condemned to Meaning* (New York: Harper & Row, 1965), where his aphorism provides the theme throughout.

8. CORING

On orthodoxy and mutual suspicion, see Eric Hoffer, *The True Believer* (New York: Mentor, 1958), p. 114.

A NEW WAY OF SEEING

The discussion of seeing and looking occurs in a chapter on seeing in Carlos Castaneda, *A Separate Reality* (New York: Simon & Schuster, 1971). The discussion of catholicity is in Walter J. Ong, S.J., *American Catholic Crossroads* (New York: Macmillan, 1959), pp. 63ff.

DEVELOPMENTAL CATHOLICITY

Robert Campbell, *Spectrum of Protestant Beliefs* (Milwaukee: Bruce, 1968), pp. viii, ix, 8.

THE PATH OF MEDITATION

The Merton summary was made at the time he commented on a collection of his works at the Bellarmine College Library, and is quoted in John J. Higgins, S.J., *Merton's Theology of Prayer* (Spencer, Mass.: Cistercian Publications, 1971), pp. xivf. See also

Eugen Rosenstock-Huessy, *I Am an Impure Thinker* (Norwich, Vt.: Argo, 1970), p. viii.

THE TASKS OF CREATION

Jakob Boehme is referred to in Gajo Petrovic, *Marx in the Mid-Twentieth Century* (Garden City, N.Y.: Doubleday, 1967), p. 189. See also Henri Lefebvre, *The Sociology of Marx* (New York: Pantheon, 1968), pp. 44ff. for comment on *poiesis*. The Goethe quotation appears in Josef Pieper, *Leisure the Basis of Culture* (New York: Mentor, 1963), p. 37. For more on *praxis,* see Petrovic, op. cit., p. 80.

HUMANISM AND PROPHECY

For the Ellul reference, see *Introducing Jacques Ellul,* edited by James Y. Holloway (Grand Rapids, Mich.: William B. Eerdmans, 1970), pp. 48ff.

CARING AND CORING

Hannah Arendt, *Between Past and Future* (Cleveland: Meridian, 1963), pp. 91ff. and especially 95.